GLOBAL
JUSTICE

GLOBAL
JUSTICE

liberation and socialism

CHE GUEVARA

Edited by María del Carmen Ariet García

Centro de Estudios
CHE GUEVARA

NEW YORK • OAKLAND • LONDON

Published by Seven Stories Press on behalf of Ocean Press, Melbourne, Australia, and the
Che Guevara Studies Center, Havana. Direct all rights inquiries and permissions questions to
rights@sevenstories.com.

Library of Congress Cataloging-in-Publication Data is on file.

ISBN 978-1-64421-156-4 (paperback)
ISBN 978-1-64421-157-1 (e-book)

Published in Spanish by Ocean Sur as
Justicia Global, ISBN 978-1-64421-168-7 (paperback);
ISBN 978-1-64421-169-4 (ebook)

9 8 7 6 5 4 3 2 1

CONTENTS

INTRODUCTION

María del Carmen Ariet García
Che Guevara Studies Center, Havana

The publication in this book of such well-known and at the same time such unique works by Ernesto Che Guevara has not been done solely for literary interest but in order to bring together his ideas, reflecting certain common themes and objectives. We also wanted to demonstrate the continuity between these works and earlier writings — many of which were conceived in different contexts but which nevertheless follow a similar line — and to indicate how Che was able to merge philosophy, politics and economics in his all encompassing, coherent revolutionary vision.

A detailed reading of these works reveals the scope of Che's decisive theoretical contribution in the historical period leading up to what could be described as his international phase. These works are, above all, the culmination of a method of work in which theory was used to solve concrete problems, a process that is not apologetic or dogmatic but rather marked by a revolutionary ethic that is both humanist and Marxist. Che Guevara was clearly "ahead of his time" as his ideas and his struggle strike a chord in the current search for global justice.

Che was a Marxist thinker who emphasized practical action. He set out to generalize his revolutionary experience, using the example of the Cuban Revolution and his experiences as a leader of that revolution to inspire other revolutionaries, especially those in the Third World. Che's legacy of speeches, conference papers, essays, articles, televised talks, interviews and letters truly express the relationship between his daily actions and his final objectives, and show how he transformed theory into a viable instrument for the revolutionary movement that would ultimately help bring about the full emancipation of humankind.

The study of the development of Che's thought cannot be divorced from the historical context in which many of his ideas first emerged — a unique and significant period. The 1960s have been labeled as "the transcendental rebellion between two existing powers of domination" and by the force and prevalence with which rebellious struggles emerged. Possibly the most significant of these struggles took place in the Third World, best symbolized by the

Cuban Revolution and the influence it had on the revolutionary movement of that time.

The impact of Che's death in October 1967, and its repercussions for an entire generation of people fighting for social change, is highlighted by the Nobel Prize winner José Saramago, who recalls:

> The clandestine portrait of Ernesto Che Guevara came to the unhappy Portugal of Salazar and Caetano. His image was the most celebrated of all, a portrait in striking tones of red and black. It became the universal image for the revolutionary dreams of the world.

In spite of the historic setback of the collapse of the socialist bloc, Che's thinking and example have been revived as a way of reestablishing continuity with genuine revolutionary socialism, which strives for full national liberation as part of a project of social change.

By focusing on a particular historical epoch, it is possible to gloss over important facts. Without losing perspective, the negative and positive aspects of that period need to be assessed.

In understanding the past, we can see the objective need for such a sharp speech as that given in Algeria on February 24, 1965, at the Afro-Asia Economic Seminar, a speech which Che's detractors have said showed his break from the Cuban Revolution. In reality, this speech included nothing that Che had not previously said about the nature of capitalism and the revolutionary struggle that would open the way for a new, socialist society.

In "Socialism and Man in Cuba," the letter sent to the Uruguayan journalist Carlos Quijano,, who was the Uruaguayan director of the magazine *Marcha*, Che felt the need, among other things, to summarize his analysis of the Cuban Revolution, its experiences and its important lessons for other countries embarking on similar struggles in the future. This historic letter—written just days after the speech in Algeria and on the eve of his incorporation into the revolutionary struggle in the Congo—discussed the question of profound social change and why certain faults and inconsistencies occurring within the socialist countries would affect the process of constructing socialism.

"Message to the Tricontinental" is one of Che's more wellknown works, published for the first time on April 16, 1967, in very different circumstances from the other pieces included in this book.

By this time Che was already fighting in Bolivia. It is included here to illustrate the continuity of Che's principles. Written in the context of struggle, he presented an analysis that responded to the issues being debated in a world full of contradictions and inconsistencies. In great detail, he outlined the tactics and strategies that should be followed in revolutionary struggle in the Third World.

Detailed study of each of the texts included in this book shows that they form the basis of Che's philosophical, economic and political strategy for a tricontinental revolution. There is an historical vision that goes beyond the immediate and under which lie the foundations of a larger project. For Che, this process began with his individual experience as a young activist that later led him to become part of a collective fight when he decided to join the revolutionary struggle in Cuba; this would later extend to his participation in the struggles of other lands.

It is essential, as part of this analysis, to emphasize that Che's intellectual development was concretized through a political practice that flowed from his ideals. Central to Che's thought and actions was a deep-seated humanism, which guided his Latin Americanism and which led him to a deeper sense of Marxism, along with a sharp anti-imperialism. This was what brought him into the Cuban Revolution and later shaped his ideas about revolutionary struggle in the Third World, guided by a revolutionary ethic as a weapon of combat and the spiritual striving for the liberation of humankind.

It is this underlying ethic reflected in Che's theory and practice that is the basis for the widespread acceptance and support of his ideals in the modern world. It makes his vision for global justice far reaching and proves that—in terms of theory—Che was ahead of his time.

If we follow the thread of Che's argument through these works, we can identify consistent themes in regard to what he considered to be determining factors in the struggle to overthrow the current order and create a new social model. Che's ideas are distinguished by the framework of the struggle for socialism, initially from the point of view of attaining power and later as a participant in the struggle. This was intensified, as has been noted, by the impending situation in so-called "real socialism" and, in particular, with the Soviet socialist bloc and the processes that slowly divorced it from its original revolutionary values.

Che thoroughly analyzed what was occurring in the socialist

world, studying the different stages of its development. He initiated for the first time in a socialist country an international debate about economics, a polemic in which he was a central protagonist. Che's ideas were further developed in his comments at different meetings and at daily work sessions, recorded in the "famous" minutes of the bimonthly meetings of the Ministry for Industry, which are full of thoughtful reflections. Che often discussed issues that were later presented in his Algeria speech, where with a clear intention he elaborated many of these ideas. In addition, he made the premonition that without an awareness of the significance of enormous problems that were accumulating, the underdeveloped world would not be able to pull itself out of stagnation.

Much has been written about the conclusions that Che reached in the 1960s. Taken out of the context of "existing socialism," they were considered to be simply heresy or a definitive rupture. Most of these evaluations failed to take into account the originality and transcendent nature of his ideas and the theoretical advances that Che made in this period, as a result of his true revolutionary practice.

Che's Marxist development allowed him to quickly develop and reformulate certain ideas. These have yet to be properly explored and as time goes on it has become even more necessary to discuss and study them, in order to give full weight to the theoretical dimension of Che's thought in its own right as well as to highlight its relevance for the present.

Our commitment to the publication of these works is based on the belief that they are important in contributing to a better understanding of Che's theoretical development. We do not aim to provide an extensive analysis of its content but rather to show succinctly the evolution and importance of Che's contribution to a genuine socialist alternative.

Another important aspect of this compilation is the connection Che established between politics and economics — and his insistence that one should not be separated from the other. It is a constant theme reinforced in all his speeches and theoretical works, without which a genuine social transformation would be impeded. Without this understanding of political economy, Che's writings would be reduced to rhetoric or a mere academic exercise.

From his essay "Political Sovereignty and Economic Independence" (1960) and his speeches at Punta del Este (1961), Geneva

(1964), the United Nations (1964) and up to his speech in Algeria (February 1965), Che presents a common argument — that the only way to achieve true national sovereignty is first through political independence and then gradually working toward economic independence. From this perspective of underdevelopment, Che was aware of the inevitability of social change. It is within this context that we can clearly see the most radical ideas that would later be incorporated into his uncompromising stand against imperialism and his call for revolution in the Third World.

There is continuity in Che's main ideas, certain invariable premises, which appear first as hypothesis and later as demonstrative elements of his theoretical scaffolding. He firmly established that it is not a case of action for action's sake that determines the course of revolutionary processes, but the accurate assessment of the relative importance of each element. In this sense, he signaled a far broader perspective in so far as he concluded that the taking of power by revolutionary forces is a worldwide objective and that the struggle for the future is the strategic element in the revolution.

Along these lines, he argued for the full participation of revolutionary forces on an international level and that the socialist world should show the way to the future. This led to the conclusion that without demonstrating solidarity and support for the under-developed world, the socialist countries would not only be appeasing the forces of reaction but would actually become accomplices to those forces.

This led Che to determine the circumstances that would result in the destruction of the status quo and the creation of a new social order. He described the principal antagonist in this struggle and the correlation between the forces of reaction and revolution. His methodology emphasized that following the conquest of political power every subsequent action must be centered on the attainment of national sovereignty, which must be based on economic independence.

Che's ideas about political sovereignty and economic independence were put forth as early as his article of March 20, 1960, cited above, where he argued that full sovereignty required a structural transformation, hence the idea that these changes would only be possible through the attainment of popular power and with the full participation of the masses in the direction that the process would take.

He spoke of tactical objectives, such as Agrarian Reform, which would in turn provide a basis for the industrialization of a country and the diversification of foreign trade. This was an issue that would permeate all of his writings and speeches on this topic. Within this framework he identified economic struggles as the primary battleground and considered it part of a war that demanded collective heroism and sacrifice of all.

He reiterated that any economic victories achieved would become key elements in pursuing the main strategic objective of national sovereignty. This line held true not only for Cuba but for the entire underdeveloped world. The power of the monopolies had to be challenged, as in general they belong to no particular country, although they all have very close ties with the United States. That is why any path to liberation must be based on a victory against the monopolies.

Che drew all these ideas together at the core of his final reflections, including his speech given at the Conference on Trade and Development in Geneva, March 25, 1964, in which he acutely outlined the essence of the problem. He warned that we live in a world divided by groups of nations representing economic, social and political tendencies that are very dissimilar and with great contradictions, such as the unequal exchange that defines economic dependence.

Even forty years after they were formulated, the issues Che was dealing with are not widely known. It is therefore perhaps surprising that his ideas have so much relevance for us today. For example, he made constant references to the role of international financial and credit organizations, which at that time were a new form of imperialist domination. As part of this analysis he wrote:

[T]he IMF acts as a custodian of the dollar for the capitalist world. The International Reconstruction and Agriculture Bank is an instrument that is used to penetrate into underdeveloped countries, and the Inter-American Development Bank fulfills this sad role in the American continent. The laws and principles that these organizations are governed by appear to be, on the surface, acting in the interests of the people they are supposedly there to help. They are promoted as safeguarding equity and reciprocity within the area of international economic relations. However, in reality they are merely subtle instruments used to perpetuate exploitation and backwardness.[1]

In retrospect, Che's central argument about unequal exchange was expressed most succinctly in his speech in Algeria, where he outlined the relationship that should exist between the development of those countries that embark on the road to independence and the cost that this represented for the socialist countries. Once more, and in a very concrete way, he outlined the principled position that needed to be adopted by the socialist world.

Che clearly defined the sacrifice that was required of the more developed socialist countries in order to assist the development of dependent countries and explained how this would involve a truly revolutionary change in international relations between the socialist countries and the underdeveloped countries on the verge of creating a new social order.

Che combined ethics, economics and politics with the express objective of explaining the new ties of solidarity and the new values that should govern the conduct of future projects for change — countering egoism and individualism with sacrifice and solidarity — as the only way to achieve not just national liberation but also liberation on a global scale.

Aware of the complexity of his arguments and the position of many socialist countries, Che consistently warned that in this struggle for freedom one could not remain indifferent toward economic issues or armed confrontations, such as that taking place in Vietnam at the time. His idea was that any victory, like any defeat, belonged to all.

Che's position was clearly defined:

> There are no borders in this struggle to the death. We cannot be indifferent to what happens anywhere in the world, because a victory by any country over imperialism is our victory, just as any country's defeat is a defeat for all of us. The practice of proletarian internationalism is not only a duty for the peoples struggling for a better future, it is also an inescapable necessity. If the imperialist enemy, the United States or any other, carries out its attack against the underdeveloped peoples and the socialist countries, elementary logic determines the need for an alliance between the underdeveloped peoples and the socialist countries. If there were no other uniting factor, the common enemy should be enough.[2]

Revolutionary humanism was integral to Che's thought. This was not merely a moral imperative but a practical and objective need of the revolutionary struggle against a common enemy — imperialism. This is why, after the overt and massive U.S. military intervention in Vietnam after 1965, Che summarized his global revolutionary strategy in the "Message to the Tricontinental," explaining that only through a common struggle could victory be attained.

Never before has Che's call to action been more relevant, despite today's different circumstances and methods. In the face of the devastating effects of global capitalism, the only solution is still one of a prolonged international confrontation, in which the peoples of the Third World continue to play a crucial role. For good reason, Che insisted that unity would be determined by the presence and support of the socialist countries. Those countries, he argued, should set aside their differences, so they would not appear weak, especially when confronting the bigger problems that faced the world.

In Che's view, the search for a solution should be guided by fundamental principles and an ethic that flowed from those principles. In this regard, he commented:

The solidarity of the progressive world with the Vietnamese people has something of the bitter irony of the plebeians cheering on the gladiators in the Roman Circus. To wish the victim success is not enough; one must share his or her fate. One must join that victim in death or in victory.[3]

It was this position that was the basis for developing a true alliance between underdeveloped peoples and socialists. It also provided a necessary bridge in the global anti-imperialist strategy and the struggle for liberation.

The world has undergone deep changes brought about in large part by the disappearance of the socialist bloc. Che's warnings about the enormous problems created by the divisions within the socialist camp were not heeded. The significant change in the international balance of power has meant that the United States has emerged as the dominant force.

Despite the significance of the global changes that have occurred and the different conjunctural situation, there is a continuity between Che's liberation theory and the progressive social movements of today that seek solutions to the most acute problems that confront the world. Within these struggles, the thoughts and examples of Che, based on a deep understanding and awareness of reality, are relevant to the current global struggle. There are those who pretend that we live in the best possible world, and that it is possible to ignore the ways in which economic models have been imposed on us—reorganizing our economies according to the recipes of large international institutions—and which have brought only misery and powerlessness. They forget that in the face of these problems other more viable and more inclusive paths will be sought.

Che's legacy of a concept of struggle for socialism from the basis of power was brought together in "Socialism and Man in Cuba." It is here that we see the beginnings of these principles, starting from his experiences in guerrilla warfare in Cuba to the creation and development of a consciousness that allowed for the emergence of other ideas with bigger goals in mind, such as, building socialist societies in the Third World.

He touched on key problems, such as the relationships between the individual and the masses; the masses, the state and the leadership; and the role of developing consciousness amongst the masses in order to achieve their full participation within the new society. He also emphasized the importance of the mechanisms required to ensure that consciousness develops alongside other social changes: moral stimulus and the new concept of work as a social task. Che's new man and woman would emerge from this new consciousness, based on new values that in turn create a new sense of ethics, which would be the foundation of a new society where new relations of solidarity predominate and an individual's daily life would correspond to broader social objectives.

The individual would become the center of the objectives and concerns in this new society that must, in essence, become "a gigantic school," establishing a perfect harmony between education and self education, the pillars of technological development that are needed in the building of a socialist society.

"Socialism and Man in Cuba" is an expression of Che's Marxist humanism, where individuals act according to concrete conditions within the process of constructing socialism. This is done in accordance with a revolutionary ethic of sacrifice and solidarity, where a balance is achieved between thought and action.

The conscious and creative action of the masses in the transition to socialism was a primary tenet of Che's Marxism, recognizing the process through which the Cuban people had achieved power, a process in which Che was himself a leader.

His main argument was that an anticapitalist revolution and achieving liberation would simultaneously represent a synthesis of humanism and a revolution in consciousness. This new political culture would be a basic requirement to creating new moral values, which would, in turn, create real changes in people's behavior.

This cannot be seen merely as a theoretical exercise. Rather, Che pointed to what he considered was the course of "existing socialism" away from revolutionary values, evident in the general stagnation that occurred as a result of the mistaken policies of domination and an increasing tendency to separate the masses from state power. The state marginalized popular participation in politics and economics within society. The results are known only too well—a nonfunctional economy and, more important still, an abandonment of the intrinsic principles of socialism and Marxism, which are truly humanist and internationalist.

Che, conscious of the implications for humanity, concluded:

> Of course there are dangers in the present situation, and not only that of dogmatism, and not only that of freezing the ties with the masses midway in the great task. There is also the danger of the weaknesses we can fall into. The way is open to infection by the germs of future corruption if a person thinks that by dedicating his or her entire life to the revolution means that, in return, one should not be distracted by such worries as that one's child lacks certain things, that one's children's shoes are worn out, that one's family lacks some necessity… The revolution is made through human beings, but individuals must forge their revolutionary spirit day by day.[4]

Aware of the enormous difficulties that this road entailed, Che concluded his letter to Quijano by commenting, "the road is long and in part unknown; we know our limitations. We will create the human being of the twenty-first century—we, ourselves."[5]

What I have highlighted is that in this volume we can see Che's intellectual audacity, ahead of its time and continuing to be relevant, even in a very different world.

The internationalization of capitalism has been characterized by an absolute power in economic relations, in terms of production as well as the dominance of the key poles of capitalism. The concrete ideological expression of this process has been the consolidation of neoliberalism.

In spite of the apparent universal character of capitalism, economic power is not an expression of the whole but the privilege of a select group of countries that control the transnationals. The rest of the countries that make up the world economy are left in a state of poverty, the role designated to them by the worldwide capitalist system.

Within this power structure, those dependent and less developed countries are subjected to international economic mechanisms dominated by the hegemonic powers. In spite of being presented as the only viable and indisputable path to the progress of humanity, globalization has many intrinsic weaknesses due to the interdependence it promotes, where the transnationals use regions and countries as instruments of their global activity. The predominant feature of globalization is the global interdependence of financial markets, which is facilitated by new information and communication technology.

The paradox of the internationalization of the world economy is that it does nothing to overcome inequality—creating as it does a form of neocolonialism. Far from being eliminated, this inequality has, in fact, been exacerbated since the disappearance of the Soviet Union and the socialist camp.

The real problem constantly confronted in the "globalized" world are the deformations brought about by an increasing differentiation between the rich and poor. Despite arguments about economic growth and increased benefits for all, globalization has created widespread unemployment and social exclusion.

Another distinguishing feature of globalization has been selective economic programs, such as the Treaty on Free Trade in the Americas. This treaty is nothing more than a way for the United States to dominate Latin America—selectively and gradually incorporating the countries with the greatest potential—as part of its geopolitical and geo-economic policy.

The economic policies designed for Latin American countries are in direct response to the domestic political needs of the United States and do not take into account the economic needs of Latin

America, which has long been characterized by its incongruity and lack of sustainable regional development. Another typical example of this is the African continent, which is currently facing a real threat of extinction of its population, due to its exclusion from the prioritized zones of influence.

Our current "globalized" world generates a permanent sense of insecurity and deep sense of demoralization, which is directly linked to the lack of solidarity and the destruction of the social bases that represent the cultural gains made by humanity. Never before has this cultural production been so threatened by the commercial monopoly of literature, in a process that sees profit as the only measure.

This is another reflection of the way in which Che was consistently ahead of his time. It is now nearly 40 years since his speech at the Punta del Este Conference in August 1961 where he denounced U.S. plans to impose a cultural model for Latin American countries through the Alliance for Progress. He pointed out:

> ...they are attempting, distinguished delegates, to establish a cultural common market, organized, managed, paid for and domesticated. All the culture of [Latin] America will be at the service of imperialism's propaganda plans, to demonstrate that the hunger of our peoples isn't hunger at all, but laziness. Magnificent!... Confronted with this, we reply [with]... total and absolute condemnation... [This is] an attempt by imperialism to domesticate the one thing that our peoples had saved from disaster: our national culture.[6]

This early stand by Che has resurfaced today, especially within the anti-globalization movement, which, in its search for solutions, has exposed the social costs of the brutal economic system that has been imposed on us. This movement also strives for a sense of unity and social action with the aim of preserving the common work of humanity.

It is the responsibility of us all to find the most appropriate answer, but we must not think that these solutions will be easy. In his "Message to the Tricontinental," with real vision Che pointed out:

> Everything seems to indicate that peace, that precarious peace that bears that name only because no global conflagration has occurred, is again in danger of being broken by some irreversible

and unacceptable step taken by the United States... The world panorama is one of great complexity. The task of winning liberation still lies ahead even for some countries of old Europe, sufficiently developed to experience all the contradictions of capitalism, but so weak that they can no longer follow the course of imperialism or embark on that road. In those countries the contradictions will become explosive in the coming years. But their problems, and hence their solutions, are different from those facing our dependent and economically backward peoples.[7]

In the search for an alternative path, a humanist ethic is required, especially in confronting the destructive policies that neoliberal forces continue to impose on a global level. This should be the main concern for social movements that try to counter the neoliberal tendencies toward fragmentation and individualism.

By defending the road that will lead to social and political liberation on a national and global level — without forgetting the need to break the dominant cycle of consumerism and reach a deeper cultural consciousness and awareness of our material practices and social relations — today's social movements will attain a better understanding of the vast social disaster that neoliberalism is imposing on the whole world.

Che's project for sustainable social change, beginning with the emergence of national liberation revolutions and their transition to socialism, today represents a real alternative, a guide for all those social movements that seek to create a different future.

The ongoing study of both Che's ideas and the development of his revolutionary practice — while recognizing the new challenges presented by the key problems in the world today — can contribute to the necessary adoption of new forms of struggle and their ultimate success.

In the current political climate, the final project must be an end to all domination and an unleashing of the abilities of the free human being — unburdened by egoism and individualism — who will act according to new ethical values in a fully sovereign and peaceful world. These are the weapons that we have inherited from Che, along with his internationalist call for the transformation of society — it is a call that rises above local limitations while bringing forward, even in the present, the goal of full universal liberation.

AT THE AFRO-ASIAN CONFERENCE IN ALGERIA

DEAR BROTHERS AND SISTERS:

Cuba is here at this conference to speak on behalf of the peoples of Latin America.[1] As we have emphasized on other occasions, Cuba also speaks as an underdeveloped country as well as one that is building socialism.

It is not by accident that our delegation is permitted to give its opinion here, in the circle of the peoples of Asia and Africa.[2] A common aspiration unites us in our march toward the future: the defeat of imperialism. A common past of struggle against the same enemy has united us along the road.

This is an assembly of peoples in struggle, and the struggle is developing on two equally important fronts that require all our efforts. The struggle against imperialism, for liberation from colonial or neocolonial shackles, which is being carried out by means of political weapons, arms, or a combination of the two, is not separate from the struggle against backwardness and poverty. Both are stages on the same road leading toward the creation of a new society of justice and plenty.

It is imperative to take political power and to get rid of the oppressor classes. But then the second stage of the struggle, which may be even more difficult than the first, must be faced.

Ever since monopoly capital took over the world, it has kept the greater part of humanity in poverty, dividing all the profits among the group of the most powerful countries. The standard of living in those countries is based on the extreme poverty of our countries. To raise the living standards of the underdeveloped nations, therefore, we must fight against imperialism. And each time a country is torn away from the imperialist tree, it is not only a partial battle won against the main enemy but it also contributes to the real weakening of that enemy, and is one more step toward the final victory.

There are no borders in this struggle to the death. We cannot be indifferent to what happens anywhere in the world, because a victory by any country over imperialism is our victory, just as any country's defeat is a defeat for all of us. The practice of proletarian inter-nationalism is not only a duty for the peoples struggling for a better future, it is also an inescapable necessity. If the imperialist enemy, the United States or any other, carries out its attack against the underdeveloped peoples and the socialist countries, elementary logic determines the need for an alliance between the underdeveloped peoples and the socialist countries. If there were no other uniting factor, the common enemy should be enough.[3]

Of course, these alliances cannot be made spontaneously, without discussions, without birth pangs, which sometimes can be painful.

We said that each time a country is liberated it is a defeat for the world imperialist system. But we must agree that the break is not achieved by the mere act of proclaiming independence or winning an armed victory in a revolution. It is achieved when imperialist economic domination over a people is brought to an end. Therefore, it is a matter of vital interest to the socialist countries for a real break to take place. And it is our international duty, a duty determined by our guiding ideology, to contribute our efforts to make this liberation as rapid and deep-going as possible.

A conclusion must be drawn from all this: the socialist countries must help pay for the development of countries now starting out on the road to liberation. We state it this way with no intention whatsoever of blackmail or dramatics, nor are we looking for an easy way to get closer to the Afro-Asian peoples; it is our profound conviction. Socialism cannot exist without a change in consciousness resulting in a new fraternal attitude toward humanity, both at an individual level, within the societies where socialism is being built or has been built, and on a world scale, with regard to all peoples suffering from imperialist oppression.

We believe the responsibility of aiding dependent countries must be approached in such a spirit. There should be no more talk about developing mutually beneficial trade based on prices forced on the backward countries by the law of value and the international relations of unequal exchange that result from the law of value.[4]

How can it be "mutually beneficial" to sell at world market prices the raw materials that cost the underdeveloped countries immeasurable sweat and suffering, and to buy at world market prices the machinery produced in today's big automated factories?

If we establish that kind of relation between the two groups of nations, we must agree that the socialist countries are, in a certain way, accomplices of imperialist exploitation. It can be argued that the amount of exchange with the underdeveloped countries is an insignificant part of the foreign trade of the socialist countries. That is very true, but it does not eliminate the immoral character of that exchange.

The socialist countries have the moral duty to put an end to their tacit complicity with the exploiting countries of the West. The fact that the trade today is small means nothing. In 1959 Cuba only occasionally sold sugar to some socialist bloc countries, usually through English brokers or brokers of other nationalities. Today 80 percent of Cuba's trade is with that area. All its vital supplies come from the socialist camp, and in fact it has joined that camp. We cannot say that this entrance into the socialist camp was brought about merely by the increase in trade. Nor was the increase in trade brought about by the destruction of the old structures and the adoption of the socialist form of development. Both sides of the question intersect and are interrelated.

We did not start out on the road that ends in communism foreseeing all steps as logically predetermined by an ideology advancing toward a fixed goal. The truths of socialism, plus the raw truths of imperialism, forged our people and showed them the path that we have now taken consciously. To advance toward their own complete liberation, the peoples of Asia and Africa must take the same path. They will follow it sooner or later, regardless of what modifying adjective their socialism may take today.

For us there is no valid definition of socialism other than the abolition of the exploitation of one human being by another. As long as this has not been achieved, if we think we are in the stage of building socialism but instead of ending exploitation the work of suppressing it comes to a halt—or worse, is reversed—then we cannot even speak of building socialism.[5]

We have to prepare conditions so that our brothers and sisters

can directly and consciously take the path of the complete abolition of exploitation, but we cannot ask them to take that path if we
ourselves are accomplices in that exploitation. If we were asked
what methods are used to establish fair prices, we could not answer
because we do not know the full scope of the practical problems
involved. All we know is that, after political discussions, the Soviet
Union and Cuba have signed agreements advantageous to us, by
means of which we will sell five million tons of sugar at prices set
above those of the so-called free world sugar market. The People's
Republic of China also pays those prices in buying from us.

This is only a beginning. The real task consists of setting prices
that will permit development. A great shift in ideas will be involved
in changing the order of international relations. Foreign trade
should not determine policy, but should, on the contrary, be subor-
dinated to a fraternal policy toward the peoples.

Let us briefly analyze the problem of long-term credits for developing basic industries. Frequently we find that beneficiary countries
attempt to establish an industrial base disproportionate to their
present capacity. The products will not be consumed domestically
and the country's reserves will be risked in the undertaking.

Our thinking is as follows: The investments of the socialist states
in their own territory come directly out of the state budget, and are
recovered only by use of the products throughout the entire man-
ufacturing process, down to the finished goods. We propose that
some thought be given to the possibility of making these kinds of
investments in the underdeveloped countries. In this way we could
unleash an immense force, hidden in our continents, which have
been exploited miserably but never aided in their development.
We could begin a new stage of a real international division of labor,
based not on the history of what has been done up to now but rather
on the future history of what can be done.

The states in whose territories the new investments are to be
made would have all the inherent rights of sovereign property over
them with no payment or credit involved. But they would be obli-
gated to supply agreed-upon quantities of products to the investor
countries for a certain number of years at set prices.

The method for financing the local portion of expenses incurred
by a country receiving investments of this kind also deserves study.
The supply of marketable goods on long-term credits to the govern-

ments of underdeveloped countries could be one form of aid not requiring the contribution of freely convertible hard currency.

Another difficult problem that must be solved is the mastering of technology.[6] The shortage of technicians in underdeveloped countries is well known to us all. Educational institutions and teachers are lacking. Sometimes we lack a real understanding of our needs and have not made the decision to carry out a top-priority policy of technical, cultural and ideological development.

The socialist countries should supply the aid to organize institutions for technical education. They should insist on the great importance of this and should supply technical cadres to fill the present need.

It is necessary to further emphasize this last point. The technicians who come to our countries must be exemplary. They are comrades who will face a strange environment, often one hostile to technology, with a different language and totally different customs. The technicians who take on this difficult task must be, first of all, communists in the most profound and noble sense of the word. With this single quality, plus a modicum of flexibility and organization, wonders can be achieved.

We know this can be done. Fraternal countries have sent us a certain number of technicians who have done more for the development of our country than ten institutes, and have contributed more to our friendship than ten ambassadors or one hundred diplomatic receptions.

If we could achieve the above-listed points — and if all the technology of the advanced countries could be placed within reach of the underdeveloped countries, unhampered by the present system of patents, which prevents the spread of inventions of different countries — we would progress a great deal in our common task.

Imperialism has been defeated in many partial battles. But it remains a considerable force in the world. We cannot expect its final defeat save through effort and sacrifice on the part of us all.

The proposed set of measures, however, cannot be implemented unilaterally. The socialist countries should help pay for the development of the underdeveloped countries, we agree. But the underdeveloped countries must also steel their forces to embark resolutely on the road of building a new society — whatever name one gives it — where the machine, an instrument of labor, is no longer an instrument for the exploitation of one human being by another. Nor can the confidence of the socialist countries be expected by those who play at balancing between capitalism and socialism, trying to use each force as a counterweight in order to derive certain advantages from such competition. A new policy of absolute seriousness should govern the relations between the two groups of societies. It is worth emphasizing once again that the means of production should preferably be in the hands of the state, so that the marks of exploitation may gradually disappear.

Furthermore, development cannot be left to complete improvisation. It is necessary to plan the construction of the new society. Planning is one of the laws of socialism, and without it, socialism would not exist. Without correct planning there can be no adequate guarantee that all the various sectors of a country's economy will combine harmoniously to take the leaps forward that our epoch demands.

Planning cannot be left as an isolated problem of each of our small countries, distorted in their development, possessors of some raw materials or producers of some manufactured or semi-manufactured goods, but lacking in most others.[7] From the outset, planning should take on a certain regional dimension in order to intermix the various national economies, and thus bring about integration on a basis that is truly of mutual benefit.

We believe the road ahead is full of dangers, not dangers conjured up or foreseen in the distant future by some superior mind but palpable dangers deriving from the realities besetting us. The fight against colonialism has reached its final stages, but in the present era colonial status is only a consequence of imperialist domination. As long as imperialism exists it will, by definition, exert its domination over other countries. Today that domination is called neocolonialism.

Neocolonialism developed first in South America, throughout a whole continent, and today it begins to be felt with increasing intensity in Africa and Asia. Its forms of penetration and development have different characteristics. One is the brutal form we have seen in the Congo. Brute force, without any respect or concealment whatsoever, is its extreme weapon. There is another more subtle form: penetration into countries that win political independence, linking up with the nascent local bourgeoisies, development of a parasitic bourgeois class closely allied to the interests of the former colonizers. This development is based on a certain temporary rise in the people's standard of living, because in a very backward country the simple step from feudal to capitalist relations marks a big advance, regardless of the dire consequences for the workers in the long run.

Neocolonialism has bared its claws in the Congo. That is not a sign of strength but of weakness. It had to resort to force, its extreme weapon, as an economic argument, which has generated very intense opposing reactions. But at the same time a much more subtle form of neocolonialism is being practiced in other countries of Africa and Asia. It is rapidly bringing about what some have called the South Americanization of these continents; that is, the development of a parasitic bourgeoisie that adds nothing to the national wealth of their countries but rather deposits its huge ill-gotten profits in capitalist banks abroad, and makes deals with foreign countries to reap more profits with absolute disregard for the welfare of the people.

There are also other dangers, such as competition between fraternal countries, which are politically friendly and sometimes neighbors, as both try to develop the same investments simultaneously to produce for markets that often cannot absorb the increased volume. This competition has the disadvantage of wasting energies that could be used to achieve much greater economic coordination; furthermore, it gives the imperialist monopolies room to maneuver.

When it has been impossible to carry out a given investment project with the aid of the socialist camp, there have been occasions when the project has been accomplished by signing agreements with the capitalists. Such capitalist investments have the disadvantage not only of the terms of the loans but other, much more important disadvantages as well, such as the establishment of joint ventures with a dangerous neighbor. Since these investments in general parallel those made in other states, they tend to cause divisions between friendly countries by creating economic rivalries. Furthermore, they create the dangers of corruption flowing from the constant presence of capitalism, which is very skillful in conjuring up visions of advancement and well-being to fog the minds of many people.

Some time later, prices drop in the market saturated by similar products. The affected countries are obliged to seek new loans, or to permit additional investments in order to compete. The final consequences of such a policy are the fall of the economy into the hands of the monopolies, and a slow but sure return to the past. As we see it, the only safe method for investments is direct participation by the state as the sole purchaser of the goods, limiting imperialist activity to contracts for supplies and not letting them set one foot inside our house. And here it is just and proper to take advantage of interimperialist contradictions in order to secure the least burdensome terms.

We have to watch out for "disinterested" economic, cultural and other aid that imperialism grants directly or through puppet states, which gets a better reception in some parts of the world.

If all of these dangers are not seen in time, some countries that began their task of national liberation with faith and enthusiasm may find themselves on the neocolonial road, as monopoly domination is subtly established step by step so that its effects are difficult to discern until they brutally make themselves felt.

There is a big job to be done. Immense problems confront our two worlds — that of the socialist countries and that called the Third World — problems directly concerning human beings and their welfare, and related to the struggle against the main force that bears the responsibility for our backwardness. In the face of these problems, all countries and peoples conscious of their duties, of the dangers involved in the situation, of the sacrifices required by development, must take concrete steps to cement our friendship in the two fields that can never be separated: the economic and the political. We should organize a great solid bloc that, in its turn, helps new countries to free themselves not only from the political power of imperialism but also from its economic power.

The question of liberation by armed struggle from an oppressor political power should be dealt with in accordance with the rules of proletarian internationalism. In a socialist country at war, it would be absurd to conceive of a factory manager demanding guaranteed payment before shipping to the front the tanks produced by his factory. It ought to seem no less absurd to inquire of a people fighting for liberation, or needing arms to defend its freedom, whether or not they can guarantee payment.

Arms cannot be commodities in our world. They must be delivered to the peoples asking for them to use against the common enemy, with no charge and in the quantities needed and available. That is the spirit in which the Soviet Union and the People's Republic of China have offered us their military aid. We are socialists; we constitute a guarantee of the proper utilization of those arms. But we are not the only ones, and all of us should receive the same treatment.

The reply to the ominous attacks by US imperialism against Vietnam or the Congo should be to supply those sister countries with all the defense equipment they need, and to offer them our full solidarity without any conditions whatsoever.

In the economic field we must conquer the road to development with the most advanced technology possible. We cannot set out to follow the long ascending steps from feudalism to the nuclear and automated era. That would be a road of immense and largely useless sacrifice. We have to start from technology at its current level. We have to make the great technological leap forward that will reduce the current gap between the more developed countries and ourselves. Technology must be applied to the large factories and also to a properly developed agriculture. Above all, its foundation must be technological and ideological education, with a sufficient mass base and strength to sustain the research institutes and organizations that have to be created in each country, as well as the men and women who will use the existing technology and be capable of adapting themselves to the newly mastered technology.

These cadres must have a clear awareness of their duty to the society in which they live. There cannot be adequate technological education if it is not complemented by ideological education; without technological education, in most of our countries, there cannot be an adequate foundation for industrial development, which is what determines the development of a modern society, or the most basic consumer goods and adequate schooling.

A good part of the national revenues must be spent on so-called unproductive investment in education. And priority must be given to the development of agricultural productivity. The latter has reached truly incredible levels in many capitalist countries, producing the senseless crisis of overproduction and a surplus of grain and other food products or industrial raw materials in the developed countries. While the rest of the world goes hungry, these countries have enough land and labor to produce several times over what is needed to feed the entire world.

Agriculture must be considered a fundamental pillar of our development. Therefore, a fundamental aspect of our work should be changes in the agrarian structure, and adaptation to the new technological possibilities and to the new obligations of eliminating the exploitation of human beings.

Before making costly decisions that could cause irreparable damage, a careful survey of the national territory is needed. This is one of the preliminary steps in economic research and a basic prerequisite for correct planning.

We warmly support Algeria's proposal for institutionalizing our relations. We would just like to make some supplementary suggestions:

First: in order for the union to be an instrument in the struggle against imperialism, the cooperation of Latin American countries and an alliance with the socialist countries is necessary.

Second: we should be vigilant in preserving the revolutionary character of the union, preventing the admission into it of governments or movements not identified with the general aspirations of the people, and creating mechanisms that would permit the separation from it of any government or popular movement diverging from the just road.

Third: we must advocate the establishment of new relations on an equal footing between our countries and the capitalist ones, creating a revolutionary jurisprudence to defend ourselves in case of conflict, and to give new meaning to the relations between ourselves and the rest of the world. We speak a revolutionary language and we fight honestly for the victory of that cause. But frequently we entangle ourselves in the nets of an international law created as the result of confrontations between the imperialist powers, and not by the free peoples, the just peoples, in the course of their struggles.

For example, our peoples suffer the painful pressure of foreign bases established on their territories, or they have to carry the heavy burden of massive foreign debts. The story of these throwbacks is well known to all of us. Puppet governments, governments weakened by long struggles for liberation or the operation of the laws of the capitalist market, have allowed treaties that threaten our internal stability and jeopardize our future. Now is the time to throw off the yoke, to force renegotiation of oppressive foreign debts, and to force the imperialists to abandon their bases of aggression.

I would not want to conclude these remarks, this recitation of concepts you all know, without calling the attention of this gathering to the fact that Cuba is not the only Latin American country — it is simply the only one that has the opportunity of speaking before you today. Other peoples are shedding their blood to win the rights we have. When we send our greetings from here, and from all the conferences and the places where they may be held, to the heroic peoples of Vietnam, Laos, so-called Portuguese Guinea, South Africa, or Palestine — to all exploited countries fighting for their emancipation — we must simultaneously extend our voice of friendship, our hand and our encouragement, to our fraternal peoples in Venezuela, Guatemala and Colombia, who today, arms in hand, are resolutely saying "No!" to the imperialist enemy.

Few settings from which to make this declaration are as symbolic as Algiers, one of the most heroic capitals of freedom. May the magnificent Algerian people — schooled as few others in sufferings for independence, under the decisive leadership of its party, headed by our dear *compañero* Ahmed Ben Bella — serve as an inspiration to us in this fight without quarter against world imperialism.

SOCIALISM AND MAN
IN CUBA

DEAR *COMPAÑERO:[1]*

Though belatedly, I am completing these notes in the course of my trip through Africa,[2] hoping in this way to keep my promise. I would like to do so by dealing with the theme set forth in the title above. I think it may be of interest to Uruguayan readers.

A common argument from the mouths of capitalist spokespeople, in the ideological struggle against socialism, is that socialism, or the period of building socialism into which we have entered, is characterized by the abolition of the individual for the sake of the state. I will not try to refute this argument solely on theoretical grounds but rather to establish the facts as they exist in Cuba and then add comments of a general nature. Let me begin by broadly sketching the history of our revolutionary struggle before and after the taking of power. As is well known, the exact date of the beginning of the revolutionary struggle — which would culminate in January 1959 — was July 26, 1953. A group led by Fidel Castro attacked the Moncada barracks in Oriente Province on the morning of that day. The attack was a failure; the failure became a disaster; and the survivors ended up in prison, beginning the revolutionary struggle again after they were freed by an amnesty.

In this process, in which there was only the germ of socialism, the individual was a fundamental factor. We put our trust in him — individual, specific, with a first and last name — and the triumph or failure of the mission entrusted to him depended on that individual's capacity for action.

Then came the stage of guerrilla struggle. It developed in two distinct environments: the people, the still sleeping mass that had to be mobilized; and its vanguard, the guerrillas, the motor force of the mobilization, the generator of revolutionary consciousness and militant enthusiasm. This vanguard was the catalyzing agent that created the subjective conditions necessary for victory.

Here again, in the framework of the proletarianization of our thinking, of this revolution that took place in our habits and our minds, the individual was the basic factor. Every one of the combatants of the Sierra Maestra who reached an upper rank in the revolutionary forces has a record of outstanding deeds to his or her credit. They attained their rank on this basis.

FIRST HEROIC STAGE

This was the first heroic period, and in which combatants competed for the heaviest responsibilities, for the greatest dangers, with no other satisfaction than fulfilling a duty. In our work of revolutionary education we frequently return to this instructive theme. In the attitude of our fighters could be glimpsed the man and woman of the future.[3]

On other occasions in our history the act of total dedication to the revolutionary cause was repeated. During the October [1962 missile] crisis and in the days of Hurricane Flora [in October 1963] we saw exceptional deeds of valor and sacrifice performed by an entire people.[4] Finding the method to perpetuate this heroic attitude in daily life is, from the ideological standpoint, one of our fundamental tasks.

In January 1959, the Revolutionary Government was established with the participation of various members of the treacherous bourgeoisie. The presence of the Rebel Army was the basic element constituting the guarantee of power.

Serious contradictions developed right away. In the first instance, in February 1959, these were resolved when Fidel Castro assumed leadership of the government, taking the post of prime minister. This process culminated in July of the same year with the resignation under mass pressure of President Urrutia.[5]

In the history of the Cuban Revolution there now appeared a character, well defined in its features, which would systematically reappear: the mass.

This multifaceted being is not, as is claimed, the sum of elements of the same type (reduced, moreover, to that same type by the ruling system), which acts like a flock of sheep. It is true that it follows its leaders, basically Fidel Castro, without hesitation. But the degree to which he won this trust results precisely from having interpreted the full meaning of the people's desires and aspirations, and from the sincere struggle to fulfill the promises he made.

PARTICIPATION OF THE MASSES

The mass participated in the agrarian reform and in the difficult task of administering state enterprises;[6] it went through the heroic experience of the Bay of Pigs;[7] it was hardened in the battles against various groups of bandits armed by the CIA; it lived through one of the most important decisions of modern times during the October [missile] crisis; and today it continues to work for the building of socialism.

Viewed superficially, it might appear that those who speak of the subordination of the individual to the state are right. The mass carries out with matchless enthusiasm and discipline the tasks set by the government, whether in the field of the economy, culture, defense, sports, etc.

The initiative generally comes from Fidel, or from the revolutionary leadership, and is explained to the people, who make it their own. In some cases the party and government take a local experience and generalize it, following the same procedure.

Nevertheless, the state sometimes makes mistakes. When one of these mistakes occurs, one notes a decline in collective enthusiasm due to the effect of a quantitative diminution in each of the elements that make up the mass. Work is paralyzed until it is reduced to an insignificant level. It is time to make a correction. That is what happened in March 1962, as a result of the sectarian policy imposed on the party by Aníbal Escalante.[8]

Clearly this mechanism is not enough to ensure a succession of sensible measures. A more structured connection with the mass is needed, and we must improve it in the course of the coming years. But as far as initiatives originating in the upper strata of the government are concerned, we are currently utilizing the almost intuitive method of sounding out general reactions to the great problems we confront.

In this Fidel is a master. His own special way of fusing himself with the people can be appreciated only by seeing him in action. At the great public mass meetings one can observe something like the dialogue of two tuning forks whose vibrations interact, producing new sounds. Fidel and the mass begin to vibrate together in a dialogue of growing intensity until they reach the climax in an abrupt conclusion crowned by our cry of struggle and victory.

The difficult thing to understand for someone not living through the experience of the revolution is this close dialectical unity between the individual and the mass, in which both are interrelated and, at the same time, in which the mass, as an aggregate of individuals, interacts with its leaders.

Some phenomena of this kind can be seen under capitalism, when politicians appear capable of mobilizing popular opinion. But when these are not genuine social movements — if they were, it would not be entirely correct to call them capitalist — they live only so long as the individual who inspires them, or until the harshness of capitalist society puts an end to the people's illusions.

INVISIBLE LAWS OF CAPITALISM

In capitalist society individuals are controlled by a pitiless law usually beyond their comprehension. The alienated human specimen is tied to society as a whole by an invisible umbilical cord: the law of value.[9] This law acts upon all aspects of one's life, shaping its course and destiny.

The laws of capitalism, which are blind and are invisible to ordinary people, act upon the individual without he or she being aware of it. One sees only the vastness of a seemingly infinite horizon ahead. That is how it is painted by capitalist propagandists who purport to draw a lesson from the example of Rockefeller[10] — whether or not it is true — about the possibilities of individual success. The amount of poverty and suffering required for a Rockefeller to emerge, and the amount of depravity entailed in the accumulation of a fortune of such magnitude, are left out of the picture, and it is not always possible for the popular forces to expose this clearly.

(A discussion of how the workers in the imperialist countries gradually lose the spirit of working-class internationalism due to a certain degree of complicity in the exploitation of the dependent countries, and how this at the same time weakens the combativity of the masses in the imperialist countries, would be appropriate here, but that is a theme that goes beyond the scope of these notes.)

In any case, the road to success is portrayed as beset with perils — perils that, it would seem, an individual with the proper qualities can overcome to attain the goal. The reward is seen in the distance; the way is lonely. Furthermore, it is a contest among wolves. One can win only at the cost of the failure of others.

THE INDIVIDUAL AND SOCIALISM

I would now like to try to define the individual, the actor in this strange and moving drama of the building of socialism, in a dual existence as a unique being and as a member of society.

I think the place to start is to recognize the individual's quality of incompleteness, of being an unfinished product. The vestiges of the past are brought into the present in one's consciousness, and a continual labor is necessary to eradicate them.[11] The process is two-sided. On the one hand, society acts through direct and indirect education; on the other, the individual submits to a conscious process of self-education.

The new society in formation has to compete fiercely with the past. This past makes itself felt not only in one's consciousness — in which the residue of an education systematically oriented toward isolating the individual still weighs heavily — but also through the very character of this transition period in which commodity relations still persist. The commodity is the economic cell of capitalist society. So long as it exists its effects will make themselves felt in the organization of production and, consequently, in consciousness.

Marx outlined the transition period as resulting from the explosive transformation of the capitalist system destroyed by its own contradictions. In historical reality, however, we have seen that some countries that were weak limbs on the tree of imperialism were torn off first — a phenomenon foreseen by Lenin.

In these countries, capitalism had developed sufficiently to make its effects felt by the people in one way or another. But it was not capitalism's internal contradictions that, having exhausted all possibilities, caused the system to explode. The struggle for liberation from a foreign oppressor; the misery caused by external events such as war, whose consequences privileged classes place on the backs of the exploited; liberation movements aimed at overthrowing neo-colonial regimes — these are the usual factors in unleashing this kind of explosion. Conscious action does the rest.

A complete education for social labor has not yet taken place in these countries, and wealth is far from being within the reach of the masses through the simple process of appropriation. Underdevelopment, on the one hand, and the usual flight of capital, on the other, make a rapid transition without sacrifices impossible.[12] There remains a long way to go in constructing the economic base, and the temptation is very great to follow the beaten track of material interest as the lever with which to accelerate development.

There is the danger that the forest will not be seen for the trees. The pipe dream that socialism can be achieved with the help of the dull instruments left to us by capitalism (the commodity as the economic cell, profitability, individual material interest as a lever, etc.) can lead into a blind alley. When you wind up there after having traveled a long distance with many crossroads, it is hard to figure out just where you took the wrong turn. Meanwhile, the economic foundation that has been laid has done its work of undermining the development of consciousness. To build communism it is necessary, simultaneous with the new material foundations, to build the new man and woman.

NEW CONSCIOUSNESS

That is why it is very important to choose the right instrument for mobilizing the masses. Basically, this instrument must be moral in character, without neglecting, however, a correct use of the material incentive—especially of a social character.[13]

As I have already said, in moments of great peril it is easy to muster a powerful response with moral incentives. Retaining their effectiveness, however, requires the development of a consciousness in which there is a new scale of values. Society as a whole must be converted into a gigantic school.

In rough outline this phenomenon is similar to the process by which capitalist consciousness was formed in its initial period. Capitalism uses force, but it also educates people in the system. Direct propaganda is carried out by those entrusted with explaining the inevitability of class society, either through some theory of divine origin or a mechanical theory of natural law. This lulls the masses, since they see themselves as being oppressed by an evil against which it is impossible to struggle.

Next comes hope of improvement—and in this, capitalism differed from the earlier caste systems, which offered no way out. For some people, the principle of the caste system will remain in effect: the reward for the obedient is to be transported after death to some fabulous other world where, according to the old beliefs, good people are rewarded. For other people there is this innovation: class divisions are determined by fate, but individuals can rise out of their class through work, initiative, etc. This process, and the myth of the self-made man, has to be profoundly hypocritical: it is the self-serving demonstration that a lie is the truth.

In our case, direct education acquires a much greater importance.[14] The explanation is convincing because it is true; no subterfuge is needed. It is carried on by the state's educational apparatus as a function of general, technical and ideological education through such agencies as the Ministry of Education and the party's informational apparatus. Education takes hold among the masses and the foreseen new attitude tends to become a habit. The masses continue to make it their own and to influence those who have not yet educated themselves. This is the indirect form of educating the masses, as powerful as the other, structured, one.

CONSCIOUS PROCESS OF SELF-EDUCATION

But the process is a conscious one. Individuals continually feel the impact of the new social power and perceive that they do not entirely measure up to its standards. Under the pressure of indirect education, they try to adjust themselves to a situation that they feel is right and that their own lack of development had prevented them from reaching previously. They educate themselves.

In this period of the building of socialism we can see the new man and woman being born. The image is not yet completely finished — it never will be, since the process goes forward hand in hand with the development of new economic forms.

Aside from those whose lack of education makes them take the solitary road toward satisfying their own personal ambitions, there are those — even within this new panorama of a unified march forward — who have a tendency to walk separately from the masses accompanying them. What is important, however, is that each day individuals are acquiring ever more consciousness of the need for their incorporation into society and, at the same time, of their importance as the motor of that society.

They no longer travel completely alone over lost roads toward distant aspirations. They follow their vanguard, consisting of the party, the advanced workers, the advanced individuals who walk in unity with the masses and in close communion with them.[15] The vanguard has its eyes fixed on the future and its reward, but this is not a vision of reward for the individual. The prize is the new society in which individuals will have different characteristics: the society of communist human beings.

The road is long and full of difficulties. At times we lose our way and must turn back. At other times we go too fast and separate ourselves from the masses. Sometimes we go too slow and feel the hot breath of those treading at our heels. In our zeal as revolutionaries we try to move ahead as fast as possible, clearing the way. But we know we must draw our nourishment from the mass and that it can advance more rapidly only if we inspire it by our example.

Despite the importance given to moral incentives, the fact that there remains a division into two main groups (excluding, of course, the minority that for one reason or another does not participate in the building of socialism) indicates the relative lack of development of social consciousness. The vanguard group is ideologically more advanced than the mass; the latter understands the new values, but not sufficiently. While among the former there has been a qualitative change that enables them to make sacrifices in their capacity as an advance guard, the latter see only part of the picture and must be subject to incentives and pressures of a certain intensity. This is the dictatorship of the proletariat operating not only on the defeated class but also on individuals of the victorious class.

All of this means that for total success a series of mechanisms, of revolutionary institutions, is needed.[16] Along with the image of the multitudes marching toward the future comes the concept of institutionalization as a harmonious set of channels, steps, restraints and well-oiled mechanisms which facilitate the advance, which facilitate the natural selection of those destined to march in the vanguard, and which bestow rewards on those who fulfill their duties and punishments on those who commit a crime against the society that is being built.

INSTITUTIONALIZATION OF THE REVOLUTION

This institutionalization of the revolution has not yet been achieved. We are looking for something new that will permit a complete identification between the government and the community in its entirety, something appropriate to the special conditions of the building of socialism, while avoiding at all costs transplanting the commonplaces of bourgeois democracy—such as legislative chambers, for example—into the society in formation.

Some experiments aimed at the gradual institutionalization of the revolution have been made, but without undue haste. The greatest brake has been our fear lest any appearance of formality might separate us from the masses and from the individual, which might make us lose sight of the ultimate and most important revolutionary aspiration: to see human beings liberated from their alienation.

Despite the lack of institutions, which must be overcome gradually, the masses are now making history as a conscious collective of individuals fighting for the same cause. The individual under socialism, despite apparent standardization, is more complete. Despite the lack of a perfect mechanism for it, the opportunities for self expression and making oneself felt in the social organism are infinitely greater.

It is still necessary to deepen conscious participation, individual and collective, in all the structures of management and production, and to link this to the idea of the need for technical and ideological education, so that the individual will realize that these processes are closely interdependent and their advancement is parallel. In this way the individual will reach total consciousness as a social being, which is equivalent to the full realization as a human creature, once the chains of alienation are broken.

This will be translated concretely into the reconquering of one's true nature through liberated labor, and the expression of one's own human condition through culture and art.

NEW STATUS OF WORK

In order to develop a new culture, work must acquire a new status.[17] Human-beings-as-commodities cease to exist, and a system is installed that establishes a quota for the fulfillment of one's social duty. The means of production belong to society, and the machine is merely the trench where duty is performed.

A person begins to become free from thinking of the annoying fact that one needs to work to satisfy one's animal needs. Individuals start to see themselves reflected in their work and to understand their full stature as human beings through the object created, through the work accomplished. Work no longer entails surrendering a part of one's being in the form of labor power sold, which no longer belongs to the individual, but becomes an expression of oneself, a contribution to the common life in which one is reflected, the fulfillment of one's social duty.

We are doing everything possible to give work this new status as a social duty and to link it on the one hand with the development of technology, which will create the conditions for greater freedom, and on the other hand with voluntary work based on the Marxist appreciation that one truly reaches a full human condition when no longer compelled to produce by the physical necessity to sell oneself as a commodity.

Of course, there are still coercive aspects to work, even when it is voluntary. We have not transformed all the coercion that surrounds us into conditioned reflexes of a social character and, in many cases, is still produced under the pressures of one's environment. (Fidel calls this moral compulsion.) There is still a need to undergo a complete spiritual rebirth in one's attitude toward one's own work, freed from the direct pressure of the social environment, though linked to it by new habits. That will be communism.

The change in consciousness does not take place automatically,

just as change in the economy does not take place automatically. The alterations are slow and not rhythmic; there are periods of acceleration, periods that are slower, and even retrogressions.

Furthermore, we must take into account, as I pointed out before, that we are not dealing with a period of pure transition, as Marx envisaged in his *Critique of the Gotha Program*, but rather with a new phase unforeseen by him: an initial period of the transition to communism, or of the construction of socialism. This transition is taking place in the midst of violent class struggles, and with elements of capitalism within it that obscure a complete understanding of its essence.[18]

If we add to this the scholasticism that has held back the development of Marxist philosophy and impeded a systematic treatment of the transition period, whose political economy has not yet been developed, we must agree that we are still in diapers and that it is necessary to devote ourselves to investigating all the principal characteristics of this period before elaborating an economic and political theory of greater scope.

The resulting theory will, no doubt, put great stress on the two pillars of the construction of socialism: the education of the new man and woman and the development of technology. Much remains to be done in regard to both, but delay is least excusable in regard to the concept of technology as a basic foundation, since this is not a question of going forward blindly but of following a long stretch of road already opened up by the world's more advanced countries. This is why Fidel pounds away with such insistence on the need for the technological and scientific training of our people and especially of its vanguard.

INDIVIDUALISM

In the field of ideas that do not lead to activities involving production, it is easier to see the division between material and spiritual necessity. For a long time individuals have been trying to free themselves from alienation through culture and art. While a person dies every day during the eight or more hours in which he or she functions as a commodity, individuals come to life afterward in their spiritual creations. But this remedy bears the germs of the same sickness: that of a solitary being seeking harmony with the world. One defends one's individuality, which is oppressed by the environment, and reacts to aesthetic ideas as a unique being whose aspiration is to remain immaculate. It is nothing more than an attempt to escape. The law of value is no longer simply a reflection of the relations of production; the monopoly capitalists—even while employing purely empirical methods—surround that law with a complicated scaffolding that turns it into a docile servant. The superstructure imposes a kind of art in which the artist must be educated. Rebels are subdued by the machine, and only exceptional talents may create their own work. The rest become shamefaced hirelings or are crushed.

A school of artistic experimentation is invented, which is said to be the definition of freedom; but this "experimentation" has its limits, imperceptible until there is a clash, that is, until the real problems of individual alienation arise. Meaningless anguish or vulgar amusement thus become convenient safety valves for human anxiety. The idea of using art as a weapon of protest is combated.

Those who play by the rules of the game are showered with honors—such honors as a monkey might get for performing pirouettes. The condition is that one does not try to escape from the invisible cage.

NEW IMPULSE FOR ARTISTIC EXPERIMENTATION

When the revolution took power there was an exodus of those who had been completely housebroken. The rest—whether they were revolutionaries or not—saw a new road. Artistic inquiry experienced a new impulse. The paths, however, had already been more or less laid out, and the escapist concept hid itself behind the word "freedom." This attitude was often found even among the revolutionaries themselves, a reflection in their consciousness of bourgeois idealism.

In countries that have gone through a similar process, attempts have been made to combat such tendencies with an exaggerated dogmatism. General culture became virtually taboo, and the acme of cultural aspiration was declared to be the formally exact representation of nature. This was later transformed into a mechanical representation of the social reality they wanted to show: the ideal society, almost without conflicts or contradictions, that they sought to create.

Socialism is young and has its mistakes. We revolutionaries often lack the knowledge and intellectual audacity needed to meet the task of developing the new man and woman with methods different from the conventional ones; conventional methods suffer from the influences of the society that created them. (Once again the theme of the relationship between form and content is posed.) Disorientation is widespread, and the problems of material construction absorb us. There are no artists of great authority who also have great revolutionary authority. The members of the party must take this task in hand and seek the achievement of the main goal: to educate the people.

What is sought then is simplification, something everyone can understand, something functionaries understand. True artistic experimentation ends, and the problem of general culture is reduced to assimilating the socialist present and the dead (therefore, not dangerous) past. Thus socialist realism arises upon the foundations of the art of the last century.[19]

The realistic art of the 19th century, however, also has a class character, more purely capitalist perhaps than the decadent art of the 20th century that reveals the anguish of the alienated individual. In the field of culture, capitalism has given all that it had to give, and nothing remains but the stench of a corpse, today's decadence in art.

But why try to find the only valid prescription in the frozen forms of socialist realism? We cannot counterpose "freedom" to socialist realism, because the former does not yet exist and will not exist until the complete development of the new society. We must not, from the pontifical throne of realism-at-all-costs, condemn all art forms since the first half of the 19th century, for we would then fall into the Proudhonian mistake of going back to the past, of putting a strait-jacket on the artistic expression of the people who are being born and are in the process of making themselves.

What is needed is the development of an ideological-cultural mechanism that permits both free inquiry and the uprooting of the weeds that multiply so easily in the fertilized soil of state subsidies.

In our country the error of mechanical realism has not appeared, but rather its opposite. This is because the need for the creation of a new individual has not been understood, a new human being who would represent neither the ideas of the 19th century nor those of our own decadent and morbid century.

What we must create is the human being of the twenty-first century, although this is still a subjective aspiration, not yet systematized.

This is precisely one of the fundamental objectives of our study and our work. To the extent that we achieve concrete success on a theoretical plane — or, vice versa, to the extent that we draw theoretical conclusions of a broad character on the basis of our concrete research — we will have made a valuable contribution to Marxism-Leninism, to the cause of humanity.

By reacting against the human being of the nineteenth century we have relapsed into the decadence of the twentieth century. It is not a very grave error, but we must overcome it lest we leave open the door for revisionism.

The great multitudes continue to develop. The new ideas are gaining a good momentum within society. The material possibilities for the integrated development of absolutely all members of society make the task much more fruitful. The present is a time of struggle; the future is ours.

NEW REVOLUTIONARY GENERATION

To sum up, the fault of many of our artists and intellectuals lies in their original sin: they are not true revolutionaries. We can try to graft the elm tree so that it will bear pears, but at the same time we must plant pear trees. New generations will come that will be free of original sin. The probability that great artists will appear will be greater to the degree that the field of culture and the possibilities for expression are broadened.

Our task is to prevent the current generation, torn asunder by its conflicts, from becoming perverted and from perverting new generations. We must not create either docile servants of official thought, or "scholarship students" who live at the expense of the state — practicing freedom in quotation marks. Revolutionaries will come who will sing the song of the new man and woman in the true voice of the people. This is a process that takes time.

In our society the youth and the party play a big part.[20] The former is especially important because it is the malleable clay from which the new person can be built with none of the old defects. The youth are treated in accordance with our aspirations. Their education is every day more complete, and we do not neglect their incorporation into work from the outset. Our scholarship students do physical work during their vacations or along with their studies. Work is a reward in some cases, a means of education in others, but it is never a punishment. A new generation is being born.

The party is a vanguard organization. It is made up of the best workers, who are proposed for membership by their fellow workers. It is a minority, but it has great authority because of the quality of its cadres. Our aspiration is for the party to become a mass party, but only when the masses have reached the level of the vanguard, that is, when they are educated for communism.

Our work constantly strives toward this education. The party is the living example; its cadres must teach hard work and sacrifice. By their action, they must lead the masses to the completion of the revolutionary task, which involves years of hard struggle against the difficulties of construction, class enemies, the maladies of the past, imperialism.

ROLE OF THE INDIVIDUAL

Now, I would like to explain the role played by the personality, by men and women as individuals leading the masses that make history. This is our experience; it is not a prescription.

Fidel gave the revolution its impulse in the first years, and also its leadership.[21] He always set its tone; but there is a good group of revolutionaries who are developing along the same road as the central leader. And there is a great mass that follows its leaders because it has faith in them. It has faith in those leaders because they have known how to interpret its aspirations.

It is not a matter of how many kilograms of meat one has to eat, or of how many times a year someone can go to the beach, or how many pretty things from abroad you might be able to buy with present-day wages. It is a matter of making the individual feel more complete, with much more inner wealth and much more responsibility.

People in our country know that the glorious period in which they happen to live is one of sacrifice; they are familiar with sacrifice. The first ones came to know it in the Sierra Maestra and wherever they fought; later, everyone in Cuba came to know it. Cuba is the vanguard of America and must make sacrifices because it occupies the post of advance guard, because it shows the masses of Latin America the road to full freedom.

Within the country the leadership has to carry out its vanguard role. It must be said with all sincerity that in a real revolution, to which one gives his or her all and from which one expects no material reward, the task of the vanguard revolutionary is both magnificent and agonizing.

LOVE OF LIVING HUMANITY

At the risk of seeming ridiculous, let me say that the true revolutionary is guided by great feelings of love. It is impossible to think of a genuine revolutionary lacking this quality. Perhaps it is one of the great dramas of the leader that he or she must combine a passionate spirit with a cold intelligence and make painful decisions without flinching. Our vanguard revolutionaries must idealize this love of the people, of the most sacred causes, and make it one and indivisible. They cannot descend, with small doses of daily affection, to the level where ordinary people put their love into practice.

The leaders of the revolution have children just beginning to talk, who are not learning to say "daddy"; their wives, too, must be part of the general sacrifice of their lives in order to take the revolution to its destiny. The circle of their friends is limited strictly to the circle of comrades in the revolution. There is no life outside of it.

In these circumstances one must have a large dose of humanity, a large dose of a sense of justice and truth in order to avoid dogmatic extremes, cold scholasticism, or an isolation from the masses. We must strive every day so that this love of living humanity is transformed into actual deeds, into acts that serve as examples, as a moving force.

The revolutionary, the ideological motor force of the revolution within the party, is consumed by this uninterrupted activity that comes to an end only with death, unless the construction of socialism is accomplished on a world scale. If one's revolutionary zeal is blunted when the most urgent tasks have been accomplished on a local scale and one forgets about proletarian internationalism, the revolution one leads will cease to be a driving force and sink into a comfortable drowsiness that imperialism, our irreconcilable enemy, will utilize to gain ground. Proletarian internationalism is a duty, but it is also a revolutionary necessity. This is the way we educate our people.

DANGER OF DOGMATISM

Of course there are dangers in the present situation, and not only that of dogmatism, not only that of freezing the ties with the masses midway in the great task. There is also the danger of the weaknesses we can fall into. The way is open to infection by the germs of future corruption if a person thinks that dedicating his or her entire life to the revolution means that, in return, one should not be distracted by such worries as that one's child lacks certain things, that one's children's shoes are worn out, that one's family lacks some necessity.

In our case we have maintained that our children must have, or lack, those things that the children of the ordinary citizen have or lack; our families should understand this and struggle for it to be that way. The revolution is made through human beings, but individuals must forge their revolutionary spirit day by day.

Thus we march on. At the head of the immense column—we are neither ashamed nor afraid to say it—is Fidel. After him come the best cadres of the party, and immediately behind them, so close that we feel its tremendous force, comes the people in its entirety, a solid structure of individual beings moving toward a common goal, men and women who have attained consciousness of what must be done, people who fight to escape from the realm of necessity and to enter that of freedom.

This great throng organizes itself; its organization results from its consciousness of the necessity of this organization. It is no longer a dispersed force, divisible into thousands of fragments thrown into the air like splinters from a hand grenade, trying by any means to achieve some protection from an uncertain future, in desperate struggle with their fellows.

We know that sacrifices lie ahead and that we must pay a price for the heroic fact that we are, as a nation, a vanguard. We, as leaders, know that we must pay a price for the right to say that we are at the head of a people that is at the head of America.[22] Each and every one of us readily pays his or her quota of sacrifice, conscious of being rewarded with the satisfaction of fulfilling a duty, conscious of advancing with everyone toward the new man and woman glimpsed on the horizon.

Allow me to draw some conclusions:[23]

We socialists are freer because we are more fulfilled; we are more fulfilled because we are freer.

The skeleton of our complete freedom is already formed. The flesh and the clothing are lacking; we will create them.

Our freedom and its daily sustenance are paid for in blood and sacrifice.

Our sacrifice is a conscious one: an installment paid on the freedom that we are building.

The road is long and, in part, unknown. We recognize our limitations. We will make the human being of the twenty-first century — we, ourselves.

We will forge ourselves in daily action, creating a new man and woman with a new technology.

Individuals play a role in mobilizing and leading the masses insofar as they embody the highest virtues and aspirations of the people and do not wander from the path.

Clearing the way is the vanguard group, the best among the good, the party.

The basic clay of our work is the youth; we place our hope in it and prepare it to take the banner from our hands.

If this inarticulate letter clarifies anything, it has accomplished the objective that motivated it. Accept our ritual greeting — which is like a handshake or an "Ave Maria Puríssima":

¡Patria o muerte! [Homeland or death!]

"CREATE TWO, THREE, MANY VIETNAMS"

(Message to the Tricontinental)[1]

> *"It is the hour of the furnace,*
> *and the light is all that can be seen."*
> **JOSÉ MARTÍ**

Twenty-one years have elapsed since the end of the last world conflagration, and various publications in every language are celebrating this event, symbolized by the defeat of Japan. A climate of optimism is apparent in many sectors of the different camps into which the world is divided.

Twenty-one years without a world war in these days of heightened confrontation, violent clashes and abrupt turns, appears to be a very large number. All of us declare our readiness to fight for this peace; but without analyzing its practical results (poverty, degradation, constantly increasing exploitation of enormous sectors of humanity), it is appropriate to ask whether this peace is real.

The purpose of these notes is not to write the history of the various conflicts of a local character that have followed one after another since Japan's surrender. Nor is it our task to recount the numerous and growing instances of civilian strife that have occurred in these years of supposed peace. It is enough to point to the wars in Korea and Vietnam as examples to counter the boundless optimism.[2]

In Korea, after years of ferocious struggle, the northern part of the country was left submerged in the most terrible devastation in the annals of modern war: riddled with bombs; without factories, schools or hospitals and without any kind of housing to shelter 10 million inhabitants.

Dozens of countries intervened in that war, led militarily by the United States under the false banner of the United Nations, with the massive participation of U.S. troops and the use of the conscripted South Korean people as cannon fodder. On the other side, the army and people of Korea and volunteers from the People's Republic of China received supplies and advice from the Soviet military apparatus. The United States carried out all kinds of tests of weapons of destruction, excluding thermonuclear ones, but including bacteriological and chemical weapons on a limited scale.

In Vietnam a war has been waged almost without interruption by the patriotic forces of that country against three imperialist powers: Japan, whose might plummeted after the bombings of Hiroshima and Nagasaki; France, which recovered its Indochinese colonies from that defeated country, disregarding the promises made at a time of duress; and the United States, in the latest phase of the conflict.

There have been limited confrontations on all continents, although on the Latin American continent there were for a long time only attempts at freedom struggles and military coups d'état. This was until the Cuban Revolution sounded its clarion call, signaling the importance of this region and attracting the wrath of the imperialists, compelling Cuba to defend its coasts first at the Bay of Pigs and then during the October [1962 missile] crisis. The latter incident could have touched off a war of incalculable proportions if a US-Soviet clash had occurred over the Cuban question.

Right now, however, the contradictions are clearly centered on the territories of the Indochinese peninsula and the neighboring countries. Laos and Vietnam were shaken by conflicts that ceased to be civil wars when US imperialism intervened with all its power, and the whole region became a lit fuse leading to a powder keg. In Vietnam the confrontation has taken on an extremely sharp character. It is not our intention to go into the history of this war. We will just point out some milestones.

In 1954, after the crushing defeat [of the French forces] at Dien Bien Phu, the Geneva Accords were signed, dividing Vietnam into two zones with the stipulation that elections would be held in 18 months to determine who would govern the country and how it would be reunified. The United States did not sign that document but began maneuvering to replace Emperor Bao Dai, a French puppet, with a man who suited their aims. He turned out to be Ngo Dinh Diem, whose tragic end — that of an orange squeezed dry by imperialism — is known to everyone.[3]

In the months following the signing of the accords, optimism reigned in the camp of the popular forces. They dismantled military positions of the anti-French struggle in the southern part of the country and waited for the agreement to be carried out. But the patriots soon realized that there would be no elections unless the United States felt capable of imposing its will at the ballot box, something it could not do even with all its methods of electoral fraud.

The struggles in the southern part of the country began once again, and these have been gaining in intensity. Today the US Army has grown to almost half a million invaders, while the puppet forces decline in number and, above all, have totally lost the will to fight.

It has been about two years since the United States began the systematic bombing of the Democratic Republic of Vietnam in yet another attempt to halt the fighting spirit in the south and to impose peace negotiations from a position of strength. At the beginning, the bombings were more or less isolated occurrences, carried out in the guise of reprisals for alleged provocations from the north. Then the intensity and regularity of the bombing increased, until it became one gigantic onslaught by the US Air Force carried out day after day, with the purpose of destroying every vestige of civilization in the northern zone of the country. It is only one episode in the sadly notorious escalation.

The material aims of the Yankee world have been achieved in good part despite the valiant defense put up by the Vietnamese anti-aircraft batteries, the more than 1,700 planes brought down and the aid in military supplies from the socialist camp.

This is the painful reality: Vietnam, a nation representing the aspirations and hopes for victory of the disinherited of the world, is tragically alone. This people must endure the pounding of US technology — in the south almost without defenses, in the north with some possibilities of defense — but always alone.

The solidarity of the progressive world with the Vietnamese people has something of the bitter irony of the plebeians cheering on the gladiators in the Roman Circus. To wish the victim success is not enough; one must share his or her fate. One must join that victim in death or in victory.

When we analyze the isolation of the Vietnamese we are overcome by anguish at this illogical moment in the history of humanity.[4] US imperialism is guilty of aggression. Its crimes are immense, extending over the whole world. We know this, gentlemen! But also guilty are those who, at the decisive moment, hesitated to make

Vietnam an inviolable part of socialist territory—yes, at the risk of a war of global scale, but also compelling the US imperialists to make a decision. Also guilty are those who persist in a war of insults and maneuvers, begun quite some time ago by the representatives of the two biggest powers in the socialist camp.[5]

Let us ask, seeking an honest answer: Is Vietnam isolated or not, as it tries to maintain a dangerous balancing act between the two quarrelling powers? What greatness has been shown by this people! What a stoic and courageous people! And what a lesson for the world their struggle holds.

It will be a long time before we know if President Johnson ever seriously intended to initiate some of the reforms needed by his people—to paper over the class contradictions that are appearing with explosive force and mounting frequency.[6] What is certain is that the improvements announced under the pompous title of the Great Society have gone down the drain in Vietnam. The greatest of the imperialist powers is feeling in its own bowels the bleeding inflicted by a poor, backward country; its fabulous economy is strained by the war effort. Killing has ceased to be the most comfortable business for the monopolies.

Defensive weapons, and not in sufficient number, are all these marvelous Vietnamese soldiers have besides love for their country, for their society, and an unsurpassed courage. Imperialism is bogged down in Vietnam. It sees no way out and is searching desperately for one that will permit it to emerge with dignity from the dangerous situation in which it finds itself. Furthermore, the "four points" put forward by the north and the "five" by the south have it caught in a vise, making the confrontation still more decisive.

Everything seems to indicate that peace, the precarious peace that bears that name only because no global conflagration has occurred, is again in danger of being broken by some irreversible and unacceptable step taken by the United States.

What is the role that we, the exploited of the world, must play? The peoples of three continents are watching and learning a lesson for themselves in Vietnam. Since the imperialists are using the threat of war to blackmail humanity, the correct response is not to fear war. Attack hard and without let-up at every point of confrontation—that must be the general tactic of the peoples.[7]

But in those places where this miserable peace that we endure has not been broken, what should our task be? To liberate ourselves at any price.

The world panorama is one of great complexity. The task of winning liberation still lies ahead, even for some countries of old Europe sufficiently developed to experience all the contradictions of capitalism but so weak that they can no longer follow the course of imperialism or embark on that road. In those countries the contradictions will become explosive in the coming years. But their problems, and hence their solutions, are different from those facing our dependent and economically backward peoples.

The fundamental field of imperialist exploitation covers the three backward continents — Latin America, Asia and Africa. Each country has its own characteristics, but the continents, as a whole, have their own features as well.

Latin America constitutes a more or less homogeneous whole, and in almost its entire territory US monopoly capital holds absolute primacy.[8] The puppet or — in the best of cases — weak and timid governments are unable to resist the orders of the Yankee master. The United States has reached virtually the pinnacle of its political and economic domination. There is little room left for it to advance; any change in the situation could turn into a step backward from its dominance. Its policy is to maintain its conquests. The course of action is reduced at the present time to the brutal use of force to prevent liberation movements of any kind.

Behind the slogan "We will not permit another Cuba" hides the possibility of cowardly acts of aggression they can get away with, such as the aggression against the Dominican Republic;[9] or before that, the massacre in Panama and the clear warning that Yankee troops are ready to intervene anywhere in Latin America where a change in the established order endangers their interests. This policy enjoys almost absolute impunity. Despite its lack of credibility, the OAS is a convenient mask. The ineffectiveness of the UN borders on the ridiculous or the tragic. The armies of all the countries of Latin America are ready to intervene to crush their own people. What has been formed, in fact, is the International of Crime and Betrayal.

On the other hand, the indigenous bourgeoisies have lost all capacity to oppose imperialism — if they ever had any — and are only dragged along behind it like a caboose.[10] There are no other alternatives: either a socialist revolution or a caricature of revolution.

Asia is a continent with different characteristics. The liberation struggles against a series of European colonial powers resulted in the establishment of more or less progressive governments, whose subsequent evolution has in some cases deepened the main objectives of national liberation and, in others, reverted toward pro-imperialist positions.

From the economic point of view, the United States had little to lose and much to gain in Asia. Changes work in its favor; it is struggling to displace other neocolonial powers, to penetrate new spheres of activity in the economic field, sometimes directly, sometimes utilizing Japan.

But special political conditions exist there, above all in the Indo-chinese peninsula, that give Asia characteristics of major importance and that play an important role in the global military strategy of U.S. imperialism. The latter is imposing a blockade around China utilizing at least South Korea, Japan, Taiwan, South Vietnam and Thailand.[11] This dual situation—a strategic interest as important as the military blockade of the People's Republic of China, and the ambition of U.S. capital to penetrate those big markets it does not yet dominate—makes Asia one of the most explosive places in the world today, despite the apparent stability outside of the Vietnamese area.

Belonging geographically to the Asian continent, but with its own contradictions, the Middle East is at boiling point. It is not possible to foresee what will be the outcome of the Cold War between Israel, which is backed by the imperialists, and the progressive countries of this region. It is another one of the threatening volcanoes in the world.

Africa appears almost like virgin territory for neocolonial invasion. Changes have occurred that, to a certain degree, have compelled the neocolonial powers to give up their former absolute prerogatives. But when these changes are carried out easily and without interruption, colonialism gives way to neocolonialism, with the same consequences in regard to economic domination.

The United States did not have colonies in this region and is now struggling to penetrate its partners' old private preserves. It can be said with certainty that Africa constitutes a long-term reservoir in the strategic plans of U.S. imperialism. Its current investments there are of importance only in the Union of South Africa, and it is beginning its penetration of the Congo, Nigeria and other countries, where competition between the imperialist powers that had previously been peaceful is now becoming violent. It does not yet have big interests to defend except its alleged right to intervene any place on the globe where its monopolies smell good profits or the existence of large reserves of raw materials. All this background makes it legitimate to pose the question about the possibilities for the liberation of the peoples in the short or medium term.

If we analyze Africa, we see that there are struggles of some intensity in the Portuguese colonies of Guinea, Mozambique and Angola, with particular success in Guinea and varying successes in the other two. We are also still witnessing a struggle between Lumumba's successors and the old accomplices of [Moise] Tshombe in the Congo, a struggle that appears at the moment to be leaning in favor of the latter, who have "pacified" a big part of the country for their benefit, although war is still latent.

In Rhodesia the problem is different: British imperialism used all the means at its disposal to hand over power to the white minority, which now rules the country. The conflict, from Britain's point of view, is absolutely unofficial. This Western power, with its usual diplomatic cleverness—in plain language also called hypocrisy—presents a facade of displeasure with the measures adopted by the government of Ian Smith. It is supported in this sly attitude by some Commonwealth countries that follow it, but is attacked by a good number of the countries of Black Africa, even those that are docile economic vassals of British imperialism.

In Rhodesia the situation could become highly explosive if the efforts of the Black patriots to rise up in arms were to crystallize, and if this movement were effectively supported by the neighboring African nations. But for now all these problems are being aired in bodies as innocuous as the UN, the Commonwealth or the Organization of African Unity.

Nevertheless, the political and social evolution of Africa does not lead us to foresee a continental revolutionary situation. The liberation struggles against the Portuguese must end victoriously, but Portugal signifies nothing on the imperialist roster. The confrontations of revolutionary importance are those that put the whole imperialist apparatus in check, although we will not for that reason cease struggling for the liberation of the three Portuguese colonies and for the deepening of their revolutions.

When the Black masses of South Africa or Rhodesia begin their genuine revolutionary struggle, or when the impoverished masses of a country set out against the ruling oligarchies to conquer their right to a decent life, a new era will have opened in Africa. Up to now there has been a succession of barracks coups, in which one group of officers replaces another or replaces a ruler who no longer serves their caste interests and those of the powers that control them behind the scenes. But there have been no popular upheavals. In the Congo these characteristics were fleetingly present, inspired by the memory of Lumumba, but they have been losing strength in recent months.

In Asia, as we have seen, the situation is explosive. Vietnam and Laos, where the struggle is now going on, are not the only points of friction. The same holds true for Cambodia, where at any moment the United States might launch a direct attack.[12] We should add Thailand, Malaysia and, of course, Indonesia, where we cannot believe that the final word has been spoken despite the annihilation of the Communist Party of that country after the reactionaries took power.[13] And, of course, there is the Middle East.

In Latin America, the struggle is going on arms in hand in Guatemala, Colombia, Venezuela and Bolivia, and the first outbreaks are already beginning in Brazil. Other centers of resistance have appeared and been extinguished. But almost all the countries of this continent are ripe for a struggle of the kind that, to be triumphant, cannot settle for anything less than the establishment of a government of a socialist nature. In this continent virtually only one language is spoken save for the exceptional case of Brazil, with whose people Spanish-speakers can communicate in view of the similarity between the two languages. There is such a similarity between the classes in these countries that they have an "international American" type of identification, much more so than in other continents. Language, customs, religion, a common master, unite them. The degree and forms of exploitation are similar in their effects for exploiters and exploited in a good number of countries of our America. And within it rebellion is ripening at an accelerated rate.

We may ask: This rebellion, how will it bear fruit? What kind of rebellion will it be? We have maintained for some time that given its similar characteristics, the struggle in Latin America will in due time acquire continental dimensions. It will be the scene of many great battles waged by humanity for its own liberation.

In the framework of this struggle of continental scope, those that are currently being carried on in an active way are only episodes. But they have already provided martyrs who will figure in the history of the Americas as having given their necessary quota of blood for this final stage in the struggle for the full freedom of humanity. There are the names of Commander Turcios Lima, the priest Camilo Torres, Commander Fabricio Ojeda, the Commanders Lobatón and Luis de la Puente Uceda, central figures in the revolutionary movements of Guatemala, Colombia, Venezuela and Peru.

But the active mobilization of the people creates its new leaders — César Montes and Yon Sosa are raising the banner in Guatemala; Fabio Vázquez and Marulanda are doing it in Colombia; Douglas Bravo in the western part of the country and Américo Martín in El Bachiller are leading their respective fronts in Venezuela.

New outbreaks of war will appear in these and other Latin American countries, as have already occurred in Bolivia. And they will continue to grow, with all the vicissitudes involved in this dangerous occupation of the modern revolutionary. Many will die, victims of their own errors; others will fall in the difficult combat to come; new fighters and new leaders will arise in the heat of the revolutionary struggle. The people will create their fighters and their leaders along the way in the selective framework of the war itself.

The Yankee agents of repression will increase in number. Today there are advisers in all countries where armed struggle is going on. It seems that the Peruvian army, also advised and trained by the Yankees, carried out a successful attack on the revolutionaries of that country. But if the guerrilla centers are led with sufficient political and military skill, they will become practically unbeatable and will make new Yankee reinforcements necessary. In Peru itself, with tenacity and firmness, new figures, although not yet fully known, are reorganizing the guerrilla struggle.

Little by little, the obsolete weapons that suffice to repress the small armed bands will turn into modern weapons, and the groups of advisers into US combatants, until at a certain point they find themselves obliged to send growing numbers of regular troops to secure the relative stability of a power whose national puppet army is disintegrating in the face of the guerrillas' struggles.

This is the road of Vietnam. It is the road that the peoples must follow. It is the road that Latin America will follow, with the special feature that the armed groups might establish something such as coordinating committees to make the repressive tasks of Yankee imperialism more difficult and to help their own cause.

Latin America, a continent forgotten in the recent political struggles for liberation, is beginning to make itself heard through the Tricontinental in the voice of the vanguard of its peoples: the Cuban Revolution. Latin America will have a much more important task: the creation of the world's second or third Vietnam, or second *and* third Vietnam.

We must definitely keep in mind that imperialism is a world system, the final stage of capitalism, and that it must be beaten in a great worldwide confrontation. The strategic objective of that struggle must be the destruction of imperialism.

The contribution that falls to us, the exploited and backward of the world, is to eliminate the foundations sustaining imperialism: our oppressed nations, from which capital, raw materials and cheap labor (both workers and technicians) are extracted, and to which new capital (tools of domination), arms and all kinds of goods are exported, sinking us into absolute dependence. The fundamental element of this strategic objective, then, will be the real liberation of the peoples, a liberation that will be the result of armed struggle in the majority of cases, and that, in Latin America, will almost unfailingly turn into a socialist revolution.

In focusing on the destruction of imperialism, it is necessary to identify its head, which is none other than the United States of North America. We must carry out a task of a general kind, the tactical aim of which is to draw the enemy out of their environment, compelling them to fight in places where their living habits clash with existing conditions. The adversary must not be underestimated; the US soldiers have technical ability and are backed by means of such magnitude as to make them formidable. What they lack essentially is the ideological motivation, which their most hated rivals of today — the Vietnamese soldiers — have to the highest degree. We will be able to triumph over this army only to the extent that we succeed in undermining its morale. And this is done by inflicting defeats on it and causing it repeated suffering.

This brief outline for victories, however, entails immense sacrifices by the peoples — sacrifices that must be demanded starting right now, in the light of day, and that perhaps will be less painful than those they would have to endure if we constantly avoided battle in an effort to get others to pull the chestnuts out of the fire for us.

Clearly, the last country to free itself very probably will do so without an armed struggle, and its people will be spared the suffering of a long war as cruel as imperialist wars are. But it may be impossible to avoid this struggle or its effects in a conflict of worldwide character, and that country might still suffer the same or even more. We cannot predict the future, but we must never give way to the cowardly temptation to be the standard-bearers of a people who yearn for freedom but renounce the struggle that goes with it, and who wait as if expecting it to come as a crumb of victory.

It is absolutely correct to avoid any needless sacrifice. That is why it is so important to be clear on the real possibilities that dependent Latin America has to free itself in a peaceful way. For us the answer to this question is clear: now may or may not be the right moment to start the struggle, but we can have no illusions, nor do we have a right to believe, that freedom can be won without a fight.

Moreover, the battles will not be mere street fights with stones against tear gas, or peaceful general strikes. Nor will it be the struggle of an infuriated people that destroys the repressive apparatus of the ruling oligarchies in two or three days. It will be a long, bloody struggle in which the battlefronts will be in guerrilla refuges in the cities, in the homes of the combatants (where the repression will go seeking easy victims among their families), among the massacred peasant population, in the towns or cities destroyed by the enemy's bombs. We are being pushed into this struggle. It cannot be remedied other than by preparing for it and deciding to undertake it.

The beginning will not be easy; it will be extremely difficult. All the oligarchies' repressive capacity, all its capacity for demagogy and brutality will be placed in the service of its cause.

Our mission, in the first hour, is to survive; then, to act, the perennial example of the guerrilla carrying on armed propaganda in the Vietnamese meaning of the term—that is, the propaganda of bullets, of battles waged against the enemy that are won or lost.

The great lesson of the guerrillas' invincibility is taking hold among the masses of the dispossessed, the galvanization of the national spirit, the preparation for more difficult tasks, for resistance to more violent repression. Hate as a factor in the struggle, intransigent hatred for the enemy that takes one beyond the natural limitations of a human being and converts one into an effective, violent, selective, cold, killing machine—our soldiers must be like that; a people without hate cannot triumph over a brutal enemy.

We must carry the war as far as the enemy carries it: into our enemy's home and places of recreation, making it total war. Our enemy must be prevented from having a moment's peace, a moment's quiet outside the barracks and even inside them. Attack them wherever they may be; make them feel like hunted animals wherever they go. Then their morale will begin to decline. They will become even more bestial, but the signs of the imminent decline will appear.

Let us develop genuine proletarian internationalism, with international proletarian armies.[14] Let the flag under which we fight be the sacred cause of the liberation of humanity, so that to die under the colors of Vietnam, Venezuela, Guatemala, Laos, Guinea, Colombia, Bolivia, Brazil—to mention only the current scenes of armed struggle—will be equally glorious and desirable for a Latin American, an Asian, an African and even a European.

Every drop of blood spilled in a land under whose flag one was not born is experience gathered by the survivor to be applied later in the struggle for the liberation of one's own country. And every people that liberates itself is a step forward in the battle for the liberation of one's own people.

It is time to moderate our disputes and place everything at the service of the struggle. We all know that big controversies are agitating the world that is struggling for freedom; we cannot hide that. We also know that these controversies have acquired a character and a sharpness that make dialogue and reconciliation appear extremely difficult, if not impossible. It is useless to seek ways to initiate a dialogue that those in dispute have avoided.

But the enemy is there, it strikes day after day and threatens new blows, and these blows will unite us today, tomorrow or the next day. Whoever understands this first and prepares this necessary unity will win the peoples' gratitude.

In view of the virulence and intransigence with which each side argues its case, we, the dispossessed, cannot agree with the way these differences are expressed, even when we agree with some of the positions of one or the other side, or when we agree more with the positions of one or the other side. In this time of struggle, the way in which the current differences have been aired is a weakness; but given the situation, it is an illusion to think that the matter can be resolved through words. History will either sweep away these disputes or pass its final judgment on them.

In our world in struggle, everything related to disputes around tactics and methods of action for the attainment of limited objectives must be analyzed with the respect due to the opinions of others. As for the great strategic objective — the total destruction of imperialism by means of struggle — on that we must be intransigent.

Let us sum up as follows our aspirations for victory. Destruction of imperialism by means of eliminating its strongest bulwark: the imperialist domination of the United States of North America. To take as a tactical line the gradual liberation of the peoples, one by one or in groups, involving the enemy in a difficult struggle outside his terrain; destroying his bases of support, that is, his dependent territories.

This means a long war. And, we repeat once again, a cruel war. Let no one deceive himself or herself when setting out on this course, and let no one hesitate to begin out of fear of the results it can bring upon one's own people. It is almost the only hope for victory.

We cannot evade the call of the hour. Vietnam teaches us this with its permanent lesson in heroism, its tragic daily lesson of struggle and death in order to gain the final victory.

Over there, the soldiers of imperialism encounter the discomforts of those who, accustomed to the standard of living that the United States boasts, have to confront a hostile land; the insecurity of those who cannot move without feeling that they are stepping on enemy territory; death for those who go outside their fortified compounds; the permanent hostility of the entire population. All this is provoking repercussions inside the United States. It is leading to the appearance of a factor that was attenuated by imperialism at full strength: the class struggle inside its own territory.

How close and bright would the future appear if two, three, many Vietnams flowered on the face of the globe, with their quota of death and their immense tragedies, with their daily heroism, with their repeated blows against imperialism, forcing it to disperse its forces under the lash of the growing hatred of the peoples of the world!

And if we were all capable of uniting in order to give our blows greater strength and certainty, so that the aid of all kinds to the peoples in struggle was even more effective—how great the future would be, and how near!

If we, on a small point on the map of the world, fulfill our duty and place at the disposal of the struggle whatever little we are able to give—our lives, our sacrifice—it can happen that one of these days we will draw our last breath on a bit of earth not our own, yet already ours, watered with our blood. Let it be known that we have measured the scope of our actions and that we consider ourselves no more than a part of the great army of the proletariat. But we feel proud at having learned from the Cuban Revolution and from its central leader the great lesson to be drawn from its position in this part of the world: "Of what difference are the dangers to a human being or a people, or the sacrifices they make, when what is at stake is the destiny of humanity?"

Our every action is a battle cry against imperialism and a call for the unity of the peoples against the great enemy of the human race: the United States of North America.

Wherever death may surprise us, let it be welcome if our battle cry has reached even one receptive ear, if another hand reaches out to take up our arms, and others come forward to join in our funeral dirge with the rattling of machine guns and with new cries of battle and victory.

NOTES

NOTES TO THE INTRODUCTION

1. Guevara, Ernesto Che: *Ernesto Che Guevara. Obras (1957-1967).* Casa de las Américas, La Habana, 1970, t. 2, 524. (See also *Che Guevara Reader: Writings on Politics & Revolution*, Seven Stories Press, 2022.)
2. *Ibid.,* 573.
3. *Ibid.,* 587.
4. *Ibid.,* 382-83.
5. *Ibid.,* 384.
6. *Ibid.,* 444-45.
7. *Ibid.,* 588.

NOTES ON THE SPEECH IN ALGERIA

1. Che Guevara delivered this speech at the Second Economic Seminar of Afro-Asian Solidarity, February 24, 1965. He had been touring Africa since December, after addressing the United Nations General Assembly on December 11, 1964. At this crucial time Che was preparing for his involvement in the liberation movement in the Congo, which began in April 1965. This edition of the speech incorporates for the first time corrections made by Che Guevara to the original published version of the Algiers speech. The corrections were made available from the personal archive of Che Guevara held at the Che Guevara Studies Center, Havana.
2. Che's participation in the Algiers conference reflects the relationship of Cuba to the Third World. Following the triumph of the revolution, from June to September 1959 Che embarked on a tour of the countries involved in the Bandung Pact. The Bandung Pact was the precursor to what later became the Movement of Nonaligned Countries. At the First Seminar on Planning in Algeria on July 16, 1963, Che had outlined the experiences of the Cuban Revolution, explaining that he had accepted the invitation to attend "only in order to offer a little history of our economic development, of our mistakes and successes, which might prove useful to you some time in the near future..."
3. In this speech Che defined very precisely his revolutionary thesis for the Third World and the integration of the struggle for national

liberation with socialist ideas. Che's call in Algeria on the socialist countries to give unconditional and radical support to the Third World provoked much debate. Nevertheless, history would prove him correct.

4. This definition of unequal exchange was part of Che's profound appeal made in Geneva on March 25, 1964, at the UN World Conference on Economics and Development in the Third World: "It is our duty to… draw to the attention of those present that while the status quo is maintained and justice is determined by powerful interests… it will be difficult to eliminate the prevailing tensions that endanger humankind."

5. For Che, socialism inherently meant overcoming exploitation as an essential step toward a just and humane society. Che was outspoken on this issue in debates and was often misunderstood, as was his emphasis on the need for international unity in the struggle for socialism. Che's idea was that the international socialist forces would contribute to the economic and social development of the peoples that liberated themselves.

6. Che's direct participation from 1959 to 1965 in the construction of a technological and material basis for Cuban society is strongly linked to his idea of creating the new man and woman. This is a question that he constantly returned to, considering it one of the two main pillars on which a new society would be constructed. His strategy was not only to solve immediate problems but to put in place certain structures that would secure Cuba's future scientific and technological development. He was able to advance this strategy during his time as head of the Ministry of Industry. For further reading on this topic, see his speeches: "May the Universities be Filled with Negroes, Mulattos, Workers and Peasants" (1960) and "Youth and Revolution" (1964).

7. In his efforts to understand fully the tasks in the transition to a socialist economy, Che came to see the vital role of economic planning, especially in the construction of a socialist economy in an underdeveloped country that retained elements of capitalism. Planning is necessary because it represents the first human attempt to control economic forces and characterizes this transitional period. He warned also of the trend within socialism to reform the economic system by strengthening the market, material interests and the law of value. To counter this trend, Che advocated centralized, anti-bureaucratic planning that enriched consciousness. His idea was to use conscious and organized action as the fundamental driving force of planning. For further reading see his article "The Significance of Socialist Planning" (1964) and his book *Critical Notes on Political Economy* (Ocean Press, 2007)

NOTES ON "SOCIALISM AND MAN IN CUBA"

1. This letter was sent to Carlos Quijano, director of the Uruguayan weekly publication, *Marcha*. It was published on March 12, 1965, under the title, "From Algiers, for *Marcha*. The Cuban Revolution Today." In the original edition the following editor's note was added: "Che Guevara sent this letter to *Marcha* from Algiers. This document is of the utmost importance, especially in order to understand the aims and goals of the Cuban Revolution as seen by one of the main actors in that process. The thesis presented is intended to provoke debate and, at the same time, give a new perspective on some of the foundations of current socialist thought." On November 5, 1965, the letter was republished and presented as "Exclusive: A Special Note from Che Guevara." A memo explained that *Marcha's* readers in Argentina had not been able to read the original publication, because the week that it was first published the magazine was banned in Buenos Aires. Subheadings are based on those used in the original Cuban edition. They have been added by the publisher.

2. When Che sent the letter to Quijano, he had been touring Africa since December 1964. During this African tour, Che held many meetings with African revolutionary leaders.

3. Che's concept of the man or woman of the future, as first evident in the consciousness of the combatants in Cuba's revolutionary war, was explored by his article, "Social Projections of the Rebel Army" (1959). These ideas were further developed in a speech, "The Revolutionary Doctor" (1960), where he described how Cuba was creating "a new type of individual" as a result of the revolution, because "there is nothing that can educate a person… like living through a revolution." These first ideas were deepened as part of Che's concept of the individual as a direct and conscious actor in the process of constructing socialism. This article presents a synthesis of his ideas on this question.

4. These two events in the early years of the revolution seriously tested the valor of the Cuban people in the face of disaster: first, the October [Missile] Crisis of 1962, during which the U.S. actions aimed at overthrowing the Cuban Revolution brought the world to the brink of crisis; and second, Hurricane Flora, which battered the eastern region of Cuba on October 4, 1963, resulting in over a thousand deaths. Nevertheless, Che believed that if, in fact, a new society was to be created, the masses needed to apply the same kind of consciousness in everyday activities as they had heroically displayed in such special circumstances.

5. The revolutionary victory of January 1, 1959, meant that for the first time in their history, the Cuban people attained a genuine level of popular participation in power. At first, the government was made up of figures from traditional political parties that had in one way or another supported the revolution. As measures were adopted that af-

fected the ruling classes, some dissent emerged that became the germ of the future counterrevolution, which was subsequently supported and funded by the US Government. In this early confrontation, President Manuel Urrutia was forced to resign due to public pressure when it became clear that he was presenting obstacles to measures that would benefit the population as a whole. It was at this time, with the full backing of the Cuban people, that Fidel assumed government leadership and became Prime Minister.

6. The Agrarian Reform Law of May 17, 1959, after only four months of taking power, was seen as the decisive step in fulfilling the revolutionary program proposed at Moncada in 1953. Che participated in the drafting of this new law along with other comrades proposed by the revolutionary leadership.

7. On April 17, 1961, mercenary troops that were trained and financed by the US Government, along with exile counterrevolutionary groups, invaded Cuba at the Bay of Pigs. This was part of the US plan to destabilize and ultimately overthrow the revolution. In these circumstances, the Cuban masses, who felt that they were the participants in a genuine process of social transformation, showed they were ready to defend the gains of the revolution and were able to defeat any attempt to destroy it.

8. The manifestations of sectarianism, which emerged in Cuba in the 1960s, forced the revolutionary leadership to take measures that would impede any tendency toward separating the government from the masses. As part of that leadership, Che participated in this process and analyzed on many occasions the grave consequences of such a separation. He expressed these views, for example, in the prolog he wrote for the book, *The Marxist Leninist Party*, published in 1963, where he explained: "Mistakes were made in the leadership; the party lost those essential qualities that linked them with the masses, the exercise of democratic centralism and the spirit of sacrifice… the function of the driving force of ideology is lost… [F]ortunately the old bases for this type of sectarianism have been destroyed."

9. The debate over the role of the law of value within the construction of socialism formed part of Che's outline of an economic framework and his initial ideas for the Budgetary Finance System. Due to his revolutionary humanist perspective, Che rejected any notion that included using capitalist tools or fetishes. These ideas were widely discussed in his article, "On the Concept of Value," published in the magazine *Our Industry* in October 1963. Here we see the beginning of the economic debate that Che initiated in those years and which had international significance. This polemic was conducted in his typically rigorous style. Outlining the guidelines to be followed, Che wrote: "We want to make it clear that the debate we have initiated can be invaluable for our development only if we are capable of conducting it with a strictly scientific approach and with the greatest equanimity."

10. Nelson Rockefeller, who became one of the wealthiest people in the United States, acquired his capital by a "stroke of luck," so the story

goes, when his family discovered oil. Rockefeller's economic power brought him great political influence for many years—especially with regard to Latin America policy—irrespective of who occupied the White House.

11. For Che, socialism could not exist if economics was not combined with social and political consciousness. Without an awareness of rights and duties, it would be impossible to construct a new society. This attitude would be the mechanism of socialist transition and the essential form of expressing this would be through consciousness. In this work, Che analyzed the decisive role of consciousness as opposed to the distortions produced by "real existing socialism," based on the separation of the material base of society from its superstructure. Unfortunately, historical events proved Che right, when a moral and political crisis brought about the collapse of the socialist system. Among Che's writings on this question are: "Collective Discussion: Decisions and Sole Responsibilities" (1961), "On the Construction of the Party" (1963), "Awarding Certificates for Communist Work" (1964) and "A New Attitude to Work" (1964).

12. From early on Che studied the concept of underdevelopment as he tried to define the realities of the Third World. In his article, "Cuba: Exceptional Case or Vanguard in the Struggle Against Colonialism?" (1961), Che asked: "What is 'underdevelopment'? A dwarf with an enormous head and swollen chest is 'underdeveloped,' insofar as his fragile legs and short arms do not match the rest of his anatomy. He is the product of an abnormal and distorted development. That is what we are in reality—we, who are politely referred to as 'underdeveloped.' In truth, we are colonial, semi-colonial or dependent countries, whose economies have been deformed by imperialism, which has peculiarly developed only those branches of industry or agriculture needed to complement its own complex economy."

13. Che argued that the full liberation of humankind is reached when work becomes a social duty carried out with complete satisfaction and sustained by a value system that contributes to the realization of conscious action in performing tasks. This could only be achieved by systematic education, acquired by passing through various stages in which collective action is increased. Che recognized that this would be difficult and would take time. In his desire to speed up this process, however, he developed methods of mobilizing people, bringing together their collective and individual interests. Among the most significant of these instruments were moral and material incentives, while deepening consciousness as a way of developing toward socialism. See Che's speeches: "Homage to Emulation Prize Winners" (1962) and "A New Attitude to Work" (1964).

14. In the process of creating the new man and woman, Che considered that education should be directly related to production and that it should be conducted on a daily basis as the only way for individuals to better themselves. This should also be undertaken in a collective

spirit, so that it contributed to the development of consciousness and had a greater impact. On a practical level he developed an education system within the Ministry of Industry that guaranteed a minimum level of training for workers, so that they could meet the new scientific and technolgical challenges Cuba faced.

15. Che discussed the role of the vanguard at key points. First, he defined the vanguard as a necessary element in leading the struggle and within the first line of defense. After the revolution, Che saw the vanguard as providing the real impulse for the masses to participate actively in the construction of a new society; at the head of the vanguard was the party. For this reason, Che occasionally insisted that the revolution was an accelerated process wherein those who play an active role have the right to become tired but not to become tired of being the vanguard.

16. In the period when Che was a leader, the Cuban Revolution had not yet reached a level of institutionalization so that old power structures had been completely eliminated. Nevertheless, Che argued that such institutionalization was important as a means of formalizing the integration of the masses and the vanguard. Years later in 1976, after the First Congress of the Cuban Communist Party, this task of institutionalization was codified, as an expression of the power structures created by the revolution.

17. It was Che's view that work played a crucial role in the construction of a new society. He analyzed the differences between work undertaken within a capitalist society and that which was free of alienation in a socialist society. He was aware of what was required so that workers would give their utmost and put duty and sacrifice ahead of individual gain. In a speech in 1961, Che referred to daily work as, "the most difficult, constant task that demands neither an instant violent sacrifice nor a single minute in a comrade's life in order to defend the revolution, but demands long hours every day…"

18. In order to understand the construction of socialism as a process that would eliminate the persistent roots of the previous society, Che examined the inherited relations of production. He insisted that two fundamental changes must occur as the only way to put an end to the exploitation of one human being by another and to achieve a socialist society: an increase in production and a deepening of consciousness.

19. An article such as *Socialism and Man in Cuba* could not avoid a discussion of culture, given the enormous changes that were taking place in Cuban society and power structures at the time. It was not an easy task to reflect on the concept of socialist culture in a country that was just emerging from underdevelopment and was still characterized by a neocolonial culture, imposed by a dominant class. There was a constant struggle between the values of the past and the attempt to construct an all-encompassing culture based on solidarity between people and real social justice. The struggle was made more difficult, not only by the persistence of the past culture but also by

dogmatic and authoritarian tendencies of so-called "socialist realism" in socialist countries. The antidote was to defend the best and most unique aspects of Cuban culture, avoiding excesses, and by trying to construct a culture that would express the feelings of the majority without vulgarity and schemas. This is the perspective that has been maintained in the development of revolutionary culture in Cuba, and neither neoliberalism nor globalization has been able to impede the genuine process of popular culture. This is the expression of a truly socialist society.

20. The role of the party and revolutionary youth in the construction of a new society was broadly analyzed by Che: "On the Construction of the Party," "The Marxist-Leninist Party," "To be a Young Communist" and "Youth and Revolution."

21. The harmony established between Fidel and Che from their first meeting in Mexico in 1955 represented a coming together of common ideals and a common approach to the liberation of Latin America and the building of a new society. Che referred to Fidel on many occasions in his writings and speeches, evaluating his qualities as a leader and statesman with sincere admiration and respect. Fidel reciprocated these feelings countless times. Their relationship should be investigated more deeply in order to gain a greater understanding of a transcendental historical era. For further reference see Che's *Reminiscences of the Cuban Revolutionary War* (Seven Stories Press, 2023), *Guerrilla Warfare* (Seven Stories Press, 2023), "Cuba: Historical Exceptional or Vanguard in the Anticolonial Struggle?" and "Political sovereignty and Economic Independence" (both in *Che Guevara Reader: Writings on Politics & Revolution*, Seven Stories Press, 2022), and "The Marxist-Leninist Party."

22. The study of the different stages of the Cuban Revolution—from guerrilla warfare to the achievement of revolutionary power—is systematically reflected in all Che's writings and speeches. He always highlighted the significance of Cuba's example for the rest of the Third World, as a symbol of freedom and showing the fruits of the initial stages of constructing socialism in an underdeveloped country. Aside from those already cited, see: "Farewell to the International Brigades for Voluntary Work" (1960) and "The Influence of the Cuban Revolution on Latin America" (1961)

23. Che's conclusions here summarized some of the most important concepts permeating his works, which are beautifully synthesized in this volume. These ideas provide a complete spectrum that encompasses philosophy, ethics and politics, spanning a range of complex questions.

NOTES ON "CREATE TWO, THREE, MANY VIETNAMS"

1. In January 1966, the Tricontinental Conference of Solidarity with the Peoples of Asia, Africa and Latin America took place in Cuba; it was agreed that an organization with a permanent Executive Secretariat would be

created. At the time of the conference, Che Guevara was in Tanzania, having left the Congo. The Cuban leader Manual Piñeiro, in charge of Cuba's relationship with revolutionaries in the Third World at the time, explained in 1997 that the "Message" was written by Che in a training camp in Pinar del Río in Cuba before setting out for Bolivia in 1966. Che's "Message" was published for the first time on April 16, 1967, in a special supplement which later became *Tricontinental* magazine. It was published under the title "Create Two, Three, Many Vietnams, That is the Slogan."

2. Che's first analyses of the wars in Korea and Vietnam were written in 1954 during his stay in Guatemala, which was also invaded by imperialist forces. In very different circumstances, after the triumph of the Cuban Revolution, he again discussed events in Asia. See, for example, "Solidarity with South Vietnam" (1963), the prolog of the book *War of the People, People's Army* (1964) and Che's UN speech (1964, reproduced in *Che Guevara Reader*, Seven Stories Press, 2022).

3. South Vietnamese dictator Ngo Dinh Diem was assassinated on November 1, 1963, at the instigation of Washington, which was dissatisfied at the inability of his regime to counter the military and political successes of the Vietnamese National Liberation Front.

4. For a more detailed understanding of these ideas, see Che's speech at the UN and his Algerian speech in this volume, where he proclaimed: "The ominous attack of U.S. imperialism on Vietnam or in the Congo must be met by a show of unity, gathering all our defenses to give our sister countries our unconditional solidarity."

5. On many occasions, Che referred to the differences that beset the international revolutionary movement—particularly the conflict between China and the Soviet Union—and the need to resolve those differences within the movement itself, in order to avoid damage on a wider scale. Following this line of thought, Che's theses on the Third World tried to avoid dogma and schemas. The works in this volume are an expression of Che's position on this issue.

6. President Lyndon B. Johnson was Vice-President when John F. Kennedy was assassinated on November 22, 1963. Johnson escalated US involvement in the Vietnam War and increased the level of open aggression against Cuba, providing unconditional support for counterrevolutionary organizations.

7. Che's ideas about tactics and strategy reflect a dialectical development in terms of content and objectives, tracing his experience in the Cuban revolutionary struggle up to the point where he joined the struggles in Africa and Latin America. The following works are key references: *Guerrilla Warfare* (Seven Stories Press, 2023), "Guerrilla Warfare: A Method" and "Tactics and Strategy of the Latin American Revolution" (both in *Che Guevara Reader*, Seven Stories Press, 2022), *Reminiscences of the Cuban Revolutionary War* (Seven Stories Press, 2023), and *Congo Diary* (Seven Stories Press, 2021).

8. The involvement of U.S. capital in Latin America was a major concern for Che throughout his life and was reflected in his writings. In many

of his writings and reflections Che made the connection between economics and politics and the way they function in each Latin American country. A very detailed analysis of this is found in his article "Tactics and Strategies..."

9. In April 1965 tens of thousands of U.S. troops invaded the Dominican Republic to crush a popular uprising.

10. Following his experience in the Congo, Che wrote *Reminiscences of the Revolutionary War in the Congo*, in which he detailed the most important lessons of that struggle. In the epilogue he outlined aspects of the economic, social and political realities of the region, as well as the possibilities for struggle. He described the national bourgeoisie and their dependent position within the power structures; and concluded they were a spent force, politically speaking.

11. Che's analysis about the essential realities of the Third World is fundamental to understanding his participation in the liberation struggles of different peoples. Che's "Message," written before he left for Bolivia, firmly established his political approach and the criteria on which his decision was based, echoing the views he expressed publicly at the United Nations. The content of Che's 1964 UN speech, especially his remarks about the crisis in the Middle East and Israel, is surprisingly relevant today.

12. Under President Nixon, the United States began blanket bombing in Cambodia in 1970.

13. On September 30, 1965, Indonesian General Suharto seized power and proceeded to carry out a massacre of members and supporters of the once-powerful Indonesian Communist Party. In the next several months, nearly one million people were killed.

14. The idea of internationalism on a global scale outlined by Che in his "Message" represents a synthesis of his thought and political praxis. It is this synthesis that brings us closer to the essential revolutionary, who supports the construction of a new order beginning with the taking of power through armed struggle. Che recognized that the world had reached a crossroads and that the national bourgeoisie was incapable of standing up to imperialism. Under these circumstances, the only way to liberation would be through prolonged people's war.

The Motorcycle Diaries: Notes on a Latin American Journey

Introductions by Walter Salles and Cintio Vitier
Foreword by Aleida Guevara

"The enormity of our endeavor escaped us in those moments; all we could see was the dust on the road ahead and ourselves on the bike, devouring kilometers in our flight northward," wrote a young Ernesto Guevara as he and his buddy Alberto Granado hit the road on a vintage Norton motorcycle to discover Latin America.

This is his lively and highly entertaining diary of that adventure, featuring exclusive, unpublished photos taken by the twenty-three year old Argentine medical student on his journey across a continent, and a tender foreword by Aleida Guevara offering an insightful perspective on her father—the man and the icon. (July 2021). ISBN: 978-1-64421-068-0

The Bolivian Diary

Introduction by Fidel Castro
Foreword by Camilo Guevara

Che's account of the fateful Bolivia mission that attempted to spark a continent-wide revolution. This is Che Guevara's last diary, compiled from the notebooks discovered when he was captured and executed by the Bolivian army in October 1967. It became an instant bestseller. This newly revised edition has an insightful preface by Che's eldest son Camilo, a chronology, maps, and 32 pages of rare or unpublished photos. (December 2021). ISBN: 978-1-64421-074-1

Congo Diary: Episodes of the Revolutionary War in the Congo

Foreword by Aleida Guevara
Introductions by Gabriel García Márquez and Roberto Saviano

Che Guevara's intriguing account of the revolutionary war in the Congo, filling in the missing chapter in his life. Prior to his fateful mission to Bolivia, in 1965 Che led a secret Cuban force that went to aid the African national liberation movement against the Belgian colonialists, after the assassination of Patrice Lumumba by the CIA. (November 2021). ISBN: 978-1-64421-072-7

I Embrace You with All My Revolutionary Fervor: Letters 1947–1967

Foreword by Aleida Guevara

Ernesto Che Guevara was a voyager—and thus a letter writer—for his entire adult life. The letters collected here range from letters home during his *Motorcycle Diaries* trip, to the long letter to Fidel after the success of the Cuban revolution in early 1959, from the most personal to the intensely political, revealing someone who not only thought deeply about everything he encountered, but for whom the process of social transformation was a constant companion from his youth until shortly before his death. His letters give us Che the son, the friend, the lover, the guerrilla fighter, the political leader, the philosopher, the poet. Che in these letters is often playful, funny, sometimes sarcastic, and deeply affectionate. His life was short, and these twenty years, from when he was nineteen until days before his death, show it was also incredibly rich and full. (November 2021). ISBN: 978-1-64421-244-8

Latin America Diaries:
The Sequel to *The Motorcycle Diaries*

This sequel to *The Motorcycle Diaries* includes letters, poetry, and journalism that document young Ernesto Guevara's second Latin American journey following his graduation from medical school in 1953. It reveals how the young Argentine is transformed into a militant revolutionary, ready to commit himself to the guerrilla struggle Fidel Castro and his compañeros are about to launch in Cuba against the dictatorship of General Fulgencio Batista. (September 2024). ISBN: 978-1-64421-100-7

Reminiscences of the Cuban Revolutionary War

Foreword by Aleida Guevara

Originally published a series of articles for Cuban papers, this thoroughly revised edition includes for the first time corrections made by Che himself to his diary on which he based the essays. This book also includes a foreword by Che's daughter Aleidita about how her parents met during the revolutionary war and 32 pages of photos and maps of the guerrilla campaign. (March 2025). ISBN: 978-1-64421-107-6

Che Guevara Reader:
Writings on Politics & Revolution

Edited by David Deutschmann and María del Carmen Ariet García

Recognized as one of *Time*'s "icons of the 20th century," Che Guevara became a legend in his own time and has now reemerged as a symbol of a new generation of political activists. Far more than a guerrilla strategist, Che Guevara made a profound and lasting contribution to revolutionary theory and Marxist humanism as demonstrated in this bestselling book. (June 2022). ISBN: 978-1-64421-112-0

Global Justice: Three Essays on Liberation and Socialism
Introduction by María del Carmen Ariet García
Is there an alternative to the corporate globalization and militarism that is ravaging our planet? These classic works by Ernesto Che Guevara present a revolutionary view of a different world in which human solidarity and understanding replace imperialist aggression and exploitation. (June 2024). ISBN: 978-1-64421-156-4

Guerrilla Warfare: Authoritative, Revised New Edition
Foreword by Harry "Pombo" Villegas
A bestselling classic for decades, this is Che Guevara's own incisive analysis of the Cuban revolution—a text studied by his admirers and adversaries alike. Although often regarded as a "manual" for guerrilla warfare, this book is primarily a political account of what happened in Cuba and why, explaining how a small group of dedicated fighters grew in strength with the support of the Cuban people, overcoming their limitations to defeat the US-backed dictator's army. He also analyzes why the Cuban revolution attained a "continental and international transcendence." (November 2024). ISBN: 978-1-64421-146-5

The Awakening of Latin America
Edited by María del Carmen Ariet García
In a letter to his mother in 1954, a young Ernesto Guevara wrote, "The Americas will be the theater of my adventures in a way that is much more significant than I would have believed." In *The Awakening of Latin America* we have the story of those adventures, charting Che's evolution from an impressionable young medical student to the "heroic guerrilla," assassinated in cold blood in Bolivia. Spanning seventeen years, this anthology draws on from his family's personal archives and offers the best of Che's writing: examples of his journalism, essays, speeches, letters, and even poems. As Che documents his early travels through Latin America, his involvement in the Guatemalan and Cuban revolutions, and his rise to international prominence under Fidel Castro, we see how his fervent commitment to social justice shaped and was shaped by the continent he called home.

Nearly half of this book is published for the first time and pre-dates Che's arrival in Cuba with Fidel Castro's guerrilla expedition in 1956. Also included are his notes for his unfinished book, *The Social Role of Doctors in Latin America*. (July 2024). ISBN: 978-1-64421-164-9